SILENT PORTRAITS

SILENT PORTRAITS

Stars of the Silent Screen in Historic Photographs

by Anthony Slide

For Frank Ramirez — A
remembrance of silent films —

All good wishes

Anthony Slide
— 6/4/90

Vestal Press

The Vestal Press, Ltd.
Vestal, New York 13850

Front cover photographs are of Mae Murray;
Douglas Fairbanks, Sr.; Harry Langdon with a
performing dog; and Max Linder with a cat.

Library of Congress Cataloging-in-Publication Data

Slide, Anthony.
  Silent portraits.

  Includes bibliographical references.
  1. Silent films — Pictorial works.   2. Motion pictures actors and
actresses — United States — Portraits.
I. Title.
PN1995.75.S57   1989   779'.9791430280922 [B]   89-22589
ISBN 0-911572-78-3 (alk. paper)

For Priscilla Bonner and Mary Brian

Introduction

In an age when stardom and star billing are determined by the negotiations of a performer's agent and not by public acclaim or recognition, it is sometimes difficult to appreciate the time when being a "star" had some validity. There were no "superstars" in the silent film era — that silly and pretentious term was invented in more recent years when stars became as common as the man and woman in the street, and just as indistinguishable from each other — but to have been a silent screen star meant having the adulation, adoration, and acknowledgment of millions of filmgoers.

Early film producers were quick to recognize the danger of increased salary demands that could come with star recognition, so they veiled their players in anonymity. By the same token, some actors and actresses appeared anxious not to harm their reputations as performers on the legitimate stage by acknowledging their participation in the product of a bastard art: the motion picture. Performers received no screen credit and were identified to film audiences by the companies for which they worked: Florence Lawrence became "The Biograph Girl"; Gene Gauntier, "The Kalem Girl"; Florence Turner, "The Vitagraph Girl"; etc. It was not until around 1910 that producers admitted that telling the public the names of their actors and actresses and advertising the films featuring those players created an audience for their product. In January, 1910, the Kalem Company became the first company to promote its players through theatre lobby displays; at the same time, the Vitagraph Company began sending its actors and actresses out to make personal appearances at local movie theatres and nickelodeons.

Only the American Biograph Company consistently remained unwilling to divulge the identity of its company of players that included, at one time or another, Mary Pickford, Blanche Sweet, Lillian and Dorothy Gish, Robert Harron, and Henry B. Walthall — all working under the direction of D. W. Griffith. When Carl Laemmle persuaded Florence Lawrence to leave Biograph and join his newly created Independent Motion Picture (IMP) Company in the summer of 1909, he promoted the identity of his star by mounting a publicity campaign claiming that she had been killed in St. Louis. Once that story had been widely circulated, Laemmle branded it a lie put out by his competitors. Florence Lawrence's name became a household word; she was no longer merely "The Biograph Girl." Laemmle was able to advertise her as "American's Most Popular Moving Picture Actress."

In the early 'teens, some stars, including Helen Gardner and Gene Gauntier, formed their own producing companies. The First National Circuit was created by a group of exhibitors in April, 1917, and a number of stars — Charles Chaplin, Mary Pickford, and Norma Talmadge — as well as some directors — Allan Dwan, Marshall Neilan, and Maurice Tourneur — became producers, releasing their films through the new organization. In 1919, with the creation of United Artists by Mary Pickford, Douglas Fairbanks, Charles Chaplin, and D. W. Griffith, there was no doubt that it was the star angle (and Griffith's name indicates that directors could also be stars) that sold films.

The 'teens saw the rise to fame of vamps such as Theda Bara and Louise Glaum; romantic teams such as Beverly Bayne and Francis X. Bushman or May Allison and Harold Lockwood; of dramatic stars such as Dorothy Phillips and Lillian Gish; and of the cowboy hero as exemplified by William S. Hart, "Broncho Billy" Anderson, and Tom Mix. The cinema even learned how to create stars by carefully nurturing their careers with an abundance of publicity, as Paramount did with Lila Lee and Constance Talmadge, and as William Randolph Hearst did with Marion Davies. The latter exhibited talent that enabled her to cling to stardom for almost twenty years, but other manufactured stars such as Gladys Walton, Julanne Johnston, and Hope Hampton had less impact and shorter film careers.

Long before Colleen Moore and Clara Bow were synonymous with the term "flapper," Viola Dana became the screen's first practitioner of this peculiarly twenties phenomenon with her performances in *A Chorus Girl's Romance* (1920) and *The Off-Shore Pirate* (1921), both based on stories by F. Scott Fitzgerald. While Gloria Swanson was still a Mack Sennett leading lady, Mae Murray became the first glamour heroine of the screen with her performance in *Princess Virtue* (1917).

"The star is inevitable," wrote Randolph Bartlett in a 1919 issue of *Motion Picture Magazine*. "Drama is the result of conflicting forces acting upon an individual, but can be interesting only when one is interested in the individual involved."[*] As already noted, stars formed their own production companies (most notably, Mary Pickford), although this practice was not limited to major names in the film industry. Diminutive child actress Baby Marie Osborne boasted her own company. Stars became associated with individual companies: John Bunny was always a Vitagraph comedian while Pearl White was a Pathé serial queen. Throughout the 'teens, director D. W. Griffith never recognized the star status of his players, and only Griffith's name appeared above the title. It was not until *Orphans of the Storm* (1921) that Griffith gave star billing — "With Lillian and Dorothy Gish" — under the title.

It is, unfortunately, very easy to dismiss many of the stars of the silent era as little more than mindless creatures with beautiful faces: an ego, a temperament, a vision of loveliness, and nothing more. As the cliché from *Sunset Boulevard* has it, "They had faces then."

Yes, the stars had faces — distinctive faces — but most of them also understood and excelled in the difficult art of acting in silent drama. Without question, Mary Pickford was the greatest personality of the silent screen, but her considerable range of acting talent should not be forgotten, as her 1918 vehicle *Stella Maris* clearly illustrates. Lillian Gish displayed dramatic intensity in films such as *Broken Blossoms* (1919) and *The Wind* (1928) that few actresses before or since have equalled. In comparison, few young male performers could hope to equal Robert Harron's tour-de-force acting in *Intolerance* (1916) in which he effortlessly matures from an innocent boy to an abused and worldly wise man, seemingly without having viewers consider that he was only playing a part. When remembering Robert Harron, his oft-times screen partner Mae Marsh cannot be ignored. Her roles as the Little Sister in *The Birth of a Nation* (1915) and the Dear One in *Intolerance* (1916) are as incomparable today as they were for audiences and critics more than seventy years ago.

The silent era boasted distinctive performances and distinctive faces. One recalls the wide-eyed, innocent looks of Bessie Barriscale and Enid Markey; the bedraggled innocence of Priscilla Bonner; the easy-going sensuality of Clara Bow; the regal splendor of Jetta Goudal; the cuteness of Janet Gaynor; the clean-cut, pure American good looks of "Buddy" Rogers and Mary Brian;

[*]Randolph Bartlett, "The Star Idea Versus the Star System," *Motion Picture Magazine*, August 1919, p. 37.

and the quiet dignity of Alice Terry. It was D. W. Griffith who, in 1919, identified the major stars of the screen as "people of great personalities, true emotions, and the ability to depict them before the camera."[*]

It is now more than fifty years since the cinema learned to talk and performers saw one medium of expression — pantomime — superceded by another — the spoken word. As fashions change and the world imagines that it has become more sophisticated, it is easy to sneer or snigger at the acting of the stars of the silent screen, but to do so negates an art form that was unique and required a standard of excellence that the cinema is hard pressed to meet today.

❖ ❖ ❖

More than 500 stars and featured players of the silent screen era are represented in this book from ingénues (such as Mignon Anderson) through the contract stars (such as Esther Ralston) to the veritable "queens" of the screen (such as Gloria Swanson and Pola Negri). This volume is not limited to those actors and actresses whose names appeared above the titles of films; it also includes minor featured players, comedians, and three animal stars. It *is* surprising that the silent stars had such varied abilities and looks, and that there were so many of them.

The cast of players in this book appear in alphabetical order. Following each name are birth and death years; a brief career summary; a listing of the most important films in which the performer appeared; and, where appropriate, the title of the player's autobiography. If no birth or death year is given, it is because such information is not available; it does not necessarily mean that the player is still alive.

It is hoped that this volume will serve a variety of purposes, providing not only a means of identifying players but also serving as a biographical dictionary.

Bill Doyle was particularly helpful in tracking down elusive dates. The majority of photographs are from the author's collection with additional photos provided by the Film Department of the Museum of Modern Art and Q. David Bowers. Dave Bowers and my editor at Vestal Press, Ltd., Grace Houghton, deserve thanks for helping to make this volume a reality.

[*]D. W. Griffith, "What I Demand of Movie Stars," *Motion Picture Classic*, February 1917, p. 40.

SILENT PORTRAITS

1

2

1. Jean Acker (1893–1978). Rudolph Valentino's first wife, who left him on their honeymoon night in 1919 in favor of Grace Darmond, her lesbian lover. Acker later used his name in an effort to bolster an unimportant career. Films include *Lombardi Ltd.* (1919), *Brewster's Millions* (1921), *The Woman in Chains* (1923), *Braveheart* (1925), and *The Nest* (1927).   **2. Art Acord** (1890–1931). A real cowboy who became a screen cowboy in the early years of the industry, Art Acord enjoyed his greatest success at Universal in the twenties. Films include *The Moon Riders* (1920), *The White Horseman* (1921), *In the Days of Buffalo Bill* (1922), *Pals* (1925), *The Terror* (1926), *Spurs and Saddles* (1927), and *Two Gun O'Brien* (1928).

3

4

3. Renée Adorée (1898–1933). A star thanks to her performance in *The Big Parade* (1925), but an actress of doubtful ability who seemed to teeter on the edge of being overweight. She appeared in films from 1920–1930. Films include *La Bohème* (1926), *The Exquisite Sinner* (1926), *Mr. Wu* (1927), and *The Spieler* (1928).

4. Spottiswoode Aitken (1868–1933). A venerable character actor of the 'teens and twenties remembered for his performances as Dr. Cameron in *The Birth of a Nation* (1915), Brown Eyes' father in *Intolerance* (1916), and appearances in other D. W. Griffith films. Films include *Home, Sweet Home* (1914), *The Avenging Conscience* (1914), *The Wharf Rat* (1916), *The Americano* (1917), *Nomads of the North* (1920), *Manslaughter* (1922), *The Eagle* (1925), and *Roaring Fires* (1927).

5

6

5. Mary Alden (1883–1946). Mary Alden never achieved any role as outstanding as that of the mulatto housekeeper to Austin Stoneman in *The Birth of a Nation* (1915). Her career lasted from the early 'teens into the thirties. Films include *Home, Sweet Home* (1914), *The Unpardonable Sin* (1919), *The Witching Hour* (1921), *Babbitt* (1924), *Brown of Harvard* (1926), and *The Potter* (1927).　　**6. May Allison** (1895–1989). May Allison is best remembered as a romantic film partner to Harold Lockwood from 1915–1917 and as the wife of James R. Quirk, editor of *Photoplay*. Films include *A Fool There Was* (1915; her first film), *David Harum* (1915), *The Testing of Mildred Vane* (1918), *Fair and Warmer* (1919), *The Greater Glory* (1926), and *The Telephone Girl* (1927; her last film).

7

8

7. Don Alvarado (1904–1967). "Latin Lover" leading man of late silents and early talkies who never achieved the successful level of Ricardo Cortez or Ramon Novarro despite appearances in two D. W. Griffith features. Films include *Satan in Sables* (1925), *His Jazz Bride* (1926), *Loves of Carmen* (1927), *Drums of Love* (1928), and *The Battle of the Sexes* (1928).

8. Gilbert M. "Broncho Billy" Anderson (1882–1971). The screen's first cowboy star, "Broncho Billy" Anderson made his debut in *The Great Train Robbery* (1903). He was a lumbering, unheroic-looking hero who wrote, directed, and starred in more than 300 Westerns for the Essanay Company, which he co-founded in 1907. "Broncho Billy" was the recipient of a 1957 Honorary Academy Award.

9

10

9. Mignon Anderson (1896–1983). One of the first stars of the Thanhouser Company of New Rochelle, which she joined in 1910, "Fillet Mignon" (as James Cruze dubbed her) was one of the pioneering actresses of the cinema. Films include *The Early Life of David Copperfield* (1911), *The Merchant of Venice* (1912), *The Mill on the Floss* (1915), *The City of Illusion* (1916), *Mountain Madness* (1920), and *Kisses* (1922; her last film).

10. Tsuru Aoki (1892–1961). The wife of actor Sessue Hayakawa and the only Japanese leading lady of American films, Tsuru Aoki started her career on stage at the age of eight and was active through the sixties. Films include *The Typhoon* (1914), *The Wrath of the Gods* (1914), *The Call of the East* (1917), *Five Days to Live* (1922), and *The Danger Line* (1924).   **11. Roscoe "Fatty" Arbuckle** (1849–1933). There was something obscenely offensive about "Fatty" Arbuckle that carried over into his films and, obviously, added to his problems when he was unfairly accused of the rape-murder of Virginia Rappe, an accusation which effectively ended his acting career in 1921. Arbuckle entered films with Selig in 1909; came to prominence with Keystone, 1913–1916; and after the end of his acting career was active as a director until his death. Films include *Fatty and Mabel Adrift* (1916), *The Butcher Boy* (1917), *Out West* (1918), *The Hayseed* (1919), *The Round-Up* (1921), and *Leap Year* (1921).

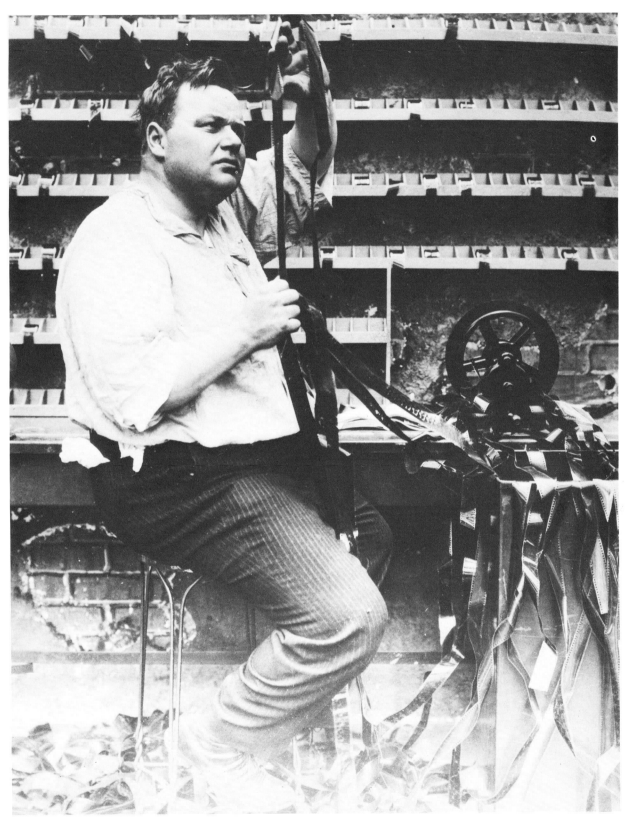

12

13

12. Richard Arlen (1900–1976). Although considered primarily a rugged hero in both silents and talkies, Richard Arlen displayed a rare emotionalism in *Wings* (1927) and *Beggars of Life* (1928). A Paramount contract star from the mid-twenties onwards, his films include *She's a Sheik* (1927), *Rolled Stockings* (1927), and *Feel My Pulse* (1928). **Margaret Armstrong**, see entry No. 157. **13. George K. Arthur** (1899–). Even in silent films, there was always something distinctively British about George K. Arthur, who came to Hollywood in 1922. He starred in and financed Josef von Sternberg's *The Salvation Hunters* (1925) and was teamed in a series of features with Karl Dane. Films include *Bardelys the Magnificent* (1926), *Irene* (1926), *Rookies* (1927), *The Student Prince in Old Heidelberg* (1927), and *Chasing Rainbows* (1930).   **14. Jean Arthur** (1905–). Minor leading lady of the silents, but a major comedienne of sound films, most notably those directed by Frank Capra. Films include *Cameo Kirby* (1923; her first film), *Biff Bang Buddy* (1924), *Seven Chances* (1925), *The Block Signal* (1926), *The Poor Nut* (1927), and *Sins of the Fathers* (1928).

14

15

15. Johnny Arthur (1883–1951). A minor purveyor of comic relief in feature films of the twenties, Johnny Arthur enjoyed a considerable sound career as a character comedian into the forties. Films include *The Unknown Purple* (1923), *Mademoiselle Midnight* (1924), *The Monster* (1925), and *On Trial* (1928).   **16. Nils Asther** (1897–1981). A star in his native Sweden and in Germany before coming to the States in the late twenties, Nils Asther was a suave leading man to Garbo in *Wild Orchids* and *The Single Standard* (both 1929), and memorable opposite Barbara Stanwyck in *The Bitter Tea of General Yen* (1933). Films include *Topsy and Eva* (1927), *Sorrell and Son* (1927), *Laugh, Clown, Laugh* (1928), and *The Cardboard Lover* (1928).

16

17

18

17. Gertrude Astor (1887–1977). Gertrude Astor's performance opposite Harry Langdon in *The Strong Man* (1926) demonstrates that here is a great, unacknowledged actress with an incredible sense of comedic timing. She usually played vamps or "other women" and was under contract to Universal from the 'teens through the mid-twenties. Films include *Beyond the Rocks* (1922), *Flaming Youth* (1923), *Alice Adams* (1923), *Kiki* (1926), and *The Cat and the Canary* (1927).

18. Mary Astor (1906–1987). A beautiful and restrained actress, equally meritorious in silent and sound films, Mary Astor was active in films from 1920 when Lillian Gish directed her in a screen test. She became a star opposite John Barrymore in *Beau Brummel* (1924). She acquired unwanted publicity in 1936 when her diaries, in which she wrote of the men with whom she had made love, were published. Films include *The Beggar Maid* (1921), *The Bright Shawl* (1923), *Puritan Passions* (1923), *Don Q, Son of Zorro* (1925), *Don Juan* (1926), *Two Arabian Knights* (1927), and more than seventy sound features. Autobiography: *My Story* (Garden City, NY: Doubleday, 1959) and *A Life on Film* (New York: Delacorte, 1967).

19

19. Agnes Ayres (1896–1940). Agnes Ayres was excellent opposite Rudolph Valentino in *The Sheik* (1921), marking the height of a career which lasted from the mid-'teens through the late twenties. Films include *The Affairs of Anatol* (1921), *Clarence* (1922), *The Ten Commandments* (1923), *The Awful Truth* (1926), and *The Donovan Affair* (1929).   **20. Lew Ayres** (1908–). Best known for his performance as Paul Baumer in *All Quiet on the Western Front* (1930) and for his noble, pacifistic stand during the Second World War, Lew Ayres was featured in one important silent film, *The Kiss* (1929), in which he played opposite Garbo. **Baby Marie Osborne**, see entry No. 385. **Baby Peggy**, see entry No. 346. **21. Olga Baclanova** (1899–1974). A Russian-born and Russian-trained actress, Olga Baclanova came to the U.S. in the mid-twenties and performed well as Lou in Josef von Sternberg's *The Docks of New York* (1928). She was even better as the leading lady in Tod Browning's *Freaks* (1932). Films include *The Man Who Laughs* (1927), *The Street of Sin* (1928), and *Forgotten Faces* (1928).

20   21

23

22

22. Helen Badgley (????–1977). With the Thanhouser Company from 1911–1917, Helen Badgley was billed from 1912 onwards as the "Thanhouser Kidlet." Films include *Brother Bob's Baby* (1911; her first film), *When the Studio Burned* (1913), *Frou Frou* (1914), *Zudora* (1914), *The Baby and the Boss* (1915), and *A Modern Monte Cristo* (1917).

23. King Baggot (1874–1948). One of the screen's first matinée idols, King Baggot entered films circa 1911 with the IMP Company. He was also a director (most notably of the 1925 production of *Tumbleweeds*) and ended his career as an extra. Publicized as "A face as well known as the man in the moon," Baggot was noted for the range of his characterizations. Films include *Ivanhoe* (1913), *Absinthe* (1913), *The Cheater* (1920), *The Forbidden Thing* (1920), and *The Butterfly Girl* (1921).

25

24

24. Leah Baird (1883–1971). A Universal and Vitagraph star of the 'teens, Leah Baird even had her own production company in the early twenties. Films include *Ivanhoe* (1913), *Neptune's Daughter* (1914), *The Heart Line* (1921), *When Husbands Deceive* (1922), and *The Primrose Path* (1925).

25. William Bakewell (1908–). An attractive "boy-next-door" type, William Bakewell was on screen from the mid-twenties through the fifties, later becoming a successful real estate broker. His first major success came with *All Quiet on the Western Front* (1930). Films include *The Last Edition* (1925), *The Heart Thief* (1927), *Harold Teen* (1928), *The Battle of the Sexes* (1928), and *The Iron Mask* (1929).

26

27

26. Mabel Ballin (1887–1958). On stage as Mabel Croft prior to her screen career and marriage to art director/director Hugo Ballin, Mabel Ballin was noted for her "chiseled and cold beauty." Films include *The Valentine Girl* (1917; her first film), *The White Heather* (1919), *The Illustrious Prince* (1919), *Jane Eyre* (1921), *East Lynne* (1921), *Vanity Fair* (1923), and *Riders of the Purple Sage* (1925).

27. George Bancroft (1882–1956). A Paramount contract star from 1925-1932, George Bancroft will always be associated with gangster roles in Josef von Sternberg's *Underworld* (1927), *The Docks of New York* (1928), and *Thunderbolt* (1925). Films include *Driven* (1923), *The Pony Express* (1925), *Old Ironsides* (1926), and *White Gold* (1927).

28

28. Vilma Banky (1903–) and **Rod La Rocque**
(1898–1969). Married in 1927 at a well-staged affair
by producer Samuel Goldwyn, the couple were
adequate performers. Vilma Banky was discovered in
her native Hungary by Goldwyn in 1925 and was
active in films through 1932. Rod La Rocque made his
film debut with Essanay in 1914 and was a Cecil B.
DeMille contract leading man from 1923–1928; active
in films through 1941. Her films include *The Eagle*
(1925), *Son of the Sheik* (1926), *The Winning of Barbara
Worth* (1926), and *The Rebel* (1932; her last film). His
films include *Paying the Piper* (1921), *Jazzmania* (1923),
The French Doll (1923), *The Ten Commandments* (1923),
Resurrection (1927), and *Meet John Doe* (1941; his last
film).   **29. Theda Bara** (1890–1955). Not the screen's
first vamp, but Theda Bara was the best known
exponent of that style and a better actress than might
be supposed. Born Theodosia Goodman, she adopted a
screen name that was an anagram of "Arab Death." A
major Fox star of the 'teens, she ended her career in the
twenties often in roles that parodied her early
successes; married director Charles Brabin. Films
include *A Fool There Was* (1914; her first film), *The Two
Orphans* (1915), *Carmen* (1915), *East Lynne* (1916),
Romeo and Juliet (1916), *Camille* (1917), *Cleopatra*
(1917), *Salome* (1918), and *Madame Mystery* (1926; her
last film).

29

30

31

30. Bessie Barriscale (1884–1965). With moonlike eyes, Bessie Barriscale made her screen debut in 1915 with *Rose of the Rancho*, in which she had also starred on stage. She quickly became one of Thomas Ince's top stars and was married to director/actor Howard Hickman. Films include *The Cup of Life* (1915), *A Corner in Colleens* (1916), *Those Who Pay* (1917), *Madam Who* (1917), *Within the Cup* (1918), and *Tangled Threads* (1919). **31. Wesley Barry** (1907–). A freckle-faced kid discovered by Marshall Neilan, Wesley Barry appeared in five features with Mary Pickford before starring in *Dinty* (1920). He later became an assistant director and producer. Films include *Rebecca of Sunnybrook Farm* (1917), *The Unpardonable Sin* (1918), *Daddy-Long-Legs* (1919), *Male and Female* (1919), *Bob Hampton of Placer* (1921), and *Penrod* (1922).

32

33

32. Ethel Barrymore (1879–1959). On stage from 1894 and a major Broadway star from 1900, Ethel Barrymore enjoyed a five-year film career in the 'teens, and then was not seen again on screen until the thirties. Films include *The Nightingale* (1914; her first film), *The Final Judgment* (1915), *The Awakening of Helena Richie* (1916), *An American Widow* (1917), *Our Mrs. McChesney* (1918), and *The Divorcée (1919)*. Autobiography: *Memories* (New York: Harper, 1955).   **33. John Barrymore** (1882–1942). A personality with a flair for melodrama and on screen from 1914–1941, John Barrymore never seemed to get over playing *Dr. Jekyll and Mr. Hyde* (1920) and repeated that performance during the rest of his career. Films include *An American Consul* (1914; his first film), *Are You a Mason?* (1915), *Raffles* (1917), *Sherlock Holmes* (1922), *Beau Brummel* (1924), *Don Juan* (1926), *Tempest* (1928), *The Beloved Rogue* (1928), and thirty-five sound features. Autobiography: *Confessions of an Actor* (Indianapolis: Bobbs-Merrill, 1926) and *We Three* (New York: Saalfield, 1935).

34

35

36

37

34. Lionel Barrymore (1878–1954). A member of the famous theatrical family, Lionel Barrymore was on stage from 1893 and in films (initially with D. W. Griffith) from 1911; somehow he always managed to appear old and crotchety even when he was not supposed to. Films include *The Power of the Press* (1914), *Wildfire* (1915), *Life's Whirlpool* (1917), *The Copperhead* (1920), *The Eternal City* (1923), *America* (1924), *The Bells* (1926), and *Drums of Love* (1928). Autobiography: *We Barrymores* (New York: Appleton-Century-Crofts, 1951).   **35. Richard Barthelmess** (1895–1963). A D. W. Griffith discovery who surpassed his performances for the master in *Broken Blossoms* (1919) and *Way Down East* (1920) with his work in *Tol'able David* (1921), his first films under a contract with Inspiration. Entered films in 1916 and ended silent era as a First National contract star from 1927. Films include *War Brides* (1916), *The Girl Who Stayed at Home* (1919), *Scarlet Days*

(1920), *The Bright Shawl* (1923), *The Enchanted Cottage* (1924), and *The Patent Leather Kid* (1927).   **36. Lina Basquette** (1907–). A child ballerina who signed a Universal contract in the mid-'teens and returned to films in the late twenties after the death of her husband, Sam Warner (married 1925–1927) of Warner Bros. fame. Films include *The Gates of Doom* (1917), *The Weaker Vessel* (1919), *Penrod* (1922), *Ranger of the North* (1927), *Serenade* (1927), *The Noose* (1928), and *Wheel of Chance* (1928).   **37. Warner Baxter** (1889–1951). Although he was on screen from the late 'teens, Warner Baxter was better known for his work during the sound era, notably in *In Old Arizona* (1929) and *42nd Street* (1933). As a silent actor, his impact was negligible. Films include *Cheated Hearts* (1921), *St. Elmo* (1923), *Those Who Dance* (1924), *The Great Gatsby* (1926), and *Singed* (1927).

38

38. Beverly Bayne (1895–1982). The leading lady of the Essanay Company in the early through mid-'teens, Beverly Bayne was usually cast opposite Francis X. Bushman, whom she later married and divorced. After her film career ended, she enjoyed a career in vaudeville and on the legitimate stage. Films include *Graustark* (1915), *Romeo and Juliet* (1916), *Red, White and Blue Blood* (1918), *Modern Marriage* (1923), and *Who Cares* (1925). **39. George Beban** (1873–1928). The stereotypical Italian of both theatre and film, George Beban re-created his greatest stage success, *The Sign of the Rose*, on screen in 1922. Films include *The Italian* (1915), *Pasquale* (1916), *The Marcellini Millions* (1917), *Hearts of Men* (1919), *One Man in a Million* (1921), and *The Greatest Love of All* (1925).

39

40

41

42

40. Barbara Bedford (1904–). Active in films through the thirties, Barbara Bedford never came close to the performance she gave in one of her first films, Maurice Tourneur's *The Last of the Mohicans* (1920). She was also William S. Hart's leading lady in *Tumbleweeds* (1925). Films include *Out of the Silent North* (1922), *Souls for Sale* (1923), *The Mad Whirl* (1925), *The Sporting Lover* (1926), *Mockery* (1927), and *The Port of Missing Girls* (1928).   **41. Noah Beery** (1882–1946). A good screen villain, particularly in the role of Sergeant Lejaune in *Beau Geste* (1926), but Noah Beery's fame was overshadowed by that of older brother Wallace. Films include *The Mormon Maid* (1917), *The Mark of Zorro* (1920), *The Spoilers* (1923), *Wanderer of the Wasteland* (1924), *The Vanishing American* (1925), and *The Dove* (1927).   **42. Wallace Beery** (1885–1949). An outrageous propensity for mugging could not hinder a career that lasted from 1913 until his death in 1949. Wallace Beery was noted for the "Sweedie" Series (1914–1915) in which he appeared in drag. Films include *Teddy at the Throttle* (1917), *Behind the Door* (1919), *Robin Hood* (1922), *Richard, the Lion-Hearted* (1923), *The Lost World* (1925), *Old Ironsides* (1926), *Beggars of Life* (1928), and fifty sound features.

43

43. Madge Bellamy (1899–). Projecting a vision of sweet innocence in a career that lasted from 1920 through the mid-thirties, Madge Bellamy's roles seldom gave her an opportunity to prove she had any acting ability. Films include *The Riddle: Woman* (1920), *Hail the Woman* (1921), *Lorna Doone* (1922), *The Iron Horse* (1924), *Lazybones* (1925), *Bertha, the Sewing Machine Girl* (1926), and *White Zombie* (1932). Autobiography: *A Darling of the Twenties* (Vestal, NY: Vestal Press, 1989).

44

45

46

44. Alma Bennett (1904–1958). Adequate leading lady of the twenties who never could, or even attempted, to outshine her leading men. Films include *The Face on the Barroom Floor* (1923), *Lilies of the Field* (1924), *The Lost World* (1925), *Don Juan's Three Nights* (1926), and *Long Pants* (1927).   **45. Belle Bennett** (1891–1932). A stunning performance in *Stella Dallas* (1925) marked the height of Belle Bennett's career, which ran from the mid-'teens until her death. Films include *East Lynne* (1925), *His Supreme Moment* (1925), *The Fourth Commandment* (1927), *The Battle of the Sexes* (1928), *Mother Machree* (1928), and *The Iron Mask* (1929).   **46. Constance Bennett** (1905–1965). The daughter of matinée idol Richard Bennett, Constance was an adequate twenties silent star who developed a far more successful career in talkies. Films include *Reckless Youth* (1922), *Cytherea* (1924), *Sally, Irene and Mary* (1925), *The Goose Woman* (1925), and *Married?* (1926).

48

47

47. Enid Bennett (1893–1969). An Australian-born actress, memorable as Lady Marian in *Robin Hood* (1922), Enid Bennett later married director Fred Niblo. Films include *The Girl Glory* (1917), *The Vamp* (1918), *The Virtuous Thief* (1919), *Hairpins* (1920), *The Courtship of Miles Standish* (1923), *The Sea Hawk* (1924), and *A Woman's Heart* (1926). **48. Andre (de) Beranger** (1893–1973). An Australian-born actor with a suave, Continental appearance — perfect in *So This is Paris* (1926), where he is first seen stripped to the waist — who began his career under contract to D. W. Griffith. Films include *The Avenging Conscience* (1914), *The Birth of a Nation* (1915), *Flirting with Fate* (1916), *Broken Blossoms* (1919), *The Bright Shawl* (1923), *Beau Brummel* (1924), *Are Parents People?* (1925), and *The Grand Duchess and the Waiter* (1926).

49

50

49. Billy Bevan (1887–1957). Australian-born and on screen from 1917 to 1952, Billy Bevan first made his mark as a comedian with Mack Sennett in 1920. Films include *Love, Honor and Behave* (1920), *A Small Town Idol* (1921), *The Extra Girl* (1923), *Lilies of the Field* (1924), *The Iron Nag* (1925), *Easy Pickings* (1927), and *Riley the Cop* (1928).

50. Francelia Billington (1895–). On screen from the mid-'teens through the thirties, Francelia Billington also worked as a camerawoman at the Reliance and Majestic Studios in 1914. Films include *Blind Husbands* (1919), *The Terror* (1920), *Hearts Are Trumps* (1920), and *What a Wife Learned* (1923).

51

53

52

51. Constance Binney (1900–). Advertised by Paramount as "The Debutante Star of Screen and Stage," Constance Binney was carefully nurtured as one of that company's Realart stars of the late 'teens and early twenties. Her sister, Faire, was also in films. Films include *Sporting Life* (1918), *Erstwhile Susan* (1919), *The Test of Honor* (1920), *39 East* (1920), *The Case of Becky* (1921), and *Midnight* (1922). **52. Carlyle Blackwell** (1884–1955). On screen from 1910, Carlyle Blackwell was an early leading man to Mary Pickford and was also active as a film star in Europe in the twenties as his career in the U. S. waned. Films include *Such a Little Queen* (1914), *The Case of Becky* (1915), *A Woman's Way* (1916), *The Road to France* (1918), and *The Restless Sea (1920)*. **53. Monte Blue** (1890–1963). A round-faced, jolly-looking actor who began his career with D. W. Griffith in 1914, Monte Blue was seen in films for more than four decades. Films include *Martyrs of the Alamo* (1915), *Jim Bludso* (1917), *M'Liss* (1918), *The Affairs of Anatol* (1921), *Orphans of the Storm* (1921), *The Marriage Circle* (1924), *So This Is Paris* (1926), and *White Shadows in the South Seas* (1928).

54

54. Betty Blythe (1893–1972). Betty Blythe came to prominence with Vitagraph in the late 'teens and will always be associated with *The Queen of Sheba* (1921). When her starring days were over, she worked as a "bit" player with one of her last appearances being in *My Fair Lady* (1964). Films include *Over the Top* (1918), *Nomads of the North* (1920), *Mother o' Mine* (1921), *The Spitfire* (1924), and *Glorious Betsy* (1928).

55

56

56. Mary Boland (1880–1965). Best known for her
work in thirties films, often opposite Charles Ruggles,
Mary Boland enjoyed an earlier screen career in the
'teens while also a major stage star (debut in 1901).
Films include *The Edge of the Abyss* (1915), *The Price of
Happiness* (1916), *Mountain Dew* (1917), *The Prodigal
Wife* (1918), *The Perfect Lover* (1919), and *His Temporary
Wife* (1920).   **57. Priscilla Bonner** (1899–). A
wistful and charming ingénue in twenties features
usually destined to suffer the anger of men or the
elements, Priscilla Bonner began her screen career in
1920 as a leading lady to Charles Ray and Will Rogers.
She was the female star of Frank Capra's first feature,
The Strong Man (1926). Films include *Homer Comes
Home* (1920; her first film), *Bob Hampton of Placer*
(1921), *Shadows* (1922), *Drusilla with a Million* (1925),
The Red Kimono (1925), *Three Bad Men* (1926), *Long
Pants* (1927), and *It* (1927).

55. Eleanor Boardman (1898–). Married to two
directors — King Vidor (for whom she made her best
films) and Harry d'Abbadie D'Arrast — Eleanor Boardman came to Hollywood after a career as a model
promoting Kodak film. Films include *Vanity Fair*
(1923), *The Circle* (1925), *Proud Flesh* (1925), *Bardelys
the Magnificent* (1926), *The Crowd* (1928), and *The Squaw
Man* (1931).

Frank Borzage
BOLTON'S MUTUAL STAR

58

58. Frank Borzage (1893–1962). A film such as *7th Heaven* (1927) represents silent filmmaking at its best, so much so that one tends to forget that its director had started as an actor with Ince in 1912 and did not begin directing until 1916. Films include *The Blood Will Tell* (1912), *A Dixie Mother* (1913), *The Wrath of the Gods* (1914), *The Typhoon* (1914), *The Pitch o' Chance* (1915), and *Jack the Pilgrim* (1916).

59

CLARA BOW.

60

59. Hobart Bosworth (1867–1943). "The Dean of the Cinema," Hobart Bosworth was a dignified presence on screen from 1909–1942. Films include *In the Sultan's Power* (1909; his first film), *The Sea Wolf* (1913), *Joan the Woman* (1916), *Behind the Door* (1919), *The Sea Lion* (1921), *My Best Girl* (1927), and *Sin Town* (1942; his last film).   **60. Clara Bow** (1906–1965). Saucy and cute, the star of Elinor Glyn's *It* (1927) and the silent screen's personification of sex appeal, Clara Bow was a better actress than her reputation might suggest. Many of her early films, beginning with a 1922 screen debut, indicate little of the sensuality that she was to display later, as witness *Down to the Sea in Ships* (1923) and the films made under her 1923 Preferred Pictures contract. A Paramount star from 1925. Films include *Black Oxen* (1924), *Dancing Mothers* (1926), *Mantrap* (1926), *Wings* (1927), *Ladies of the Mob* (1928), *The Wild Party* (1929), and *Hoopla* (1933; her last film).

61

61. John Bowers (1899–1936). John Bowers was often considered the basis for Norman Maine in *A Star is Born* because he took his own life by drowning after his career failed. He was active in films from the mid-'teens and was, at one time, married to actress Marguerite De La Motte. Films include *The Eternal Grind* (1916), *Hulda from Holland* (1916), *A Cumberland Romance* (1920), *The Sky Pilot* (1921), *Quincy Adams Sawyer* (1922), *Lorna Doone* (1922), and *Confessions of a Queen* (1925). **62. Alice Brady** (1892–1939). The daughter of theatrical impressario William Brady, Alice Brady portrayed attractive, silent heroines far removed from the scatterbrained, talkative characterizations of the thirties with which she is most often associated. Films include *As Ye Sow* (1914; her first film), *The Boss* (1915), *Betsy Ross* (1917), *The Trap* (1918), *Out of the Chorus* (1921), *Anna Ascends* (1922), and *The Snow Bride* (1923).

62

63

64

63. Sylvia Breamer (1898–1943). A contemporary writer described Australian-born Sylvia Breamer as having "dark and slumberous eyes, equally dark and slumberous hair, a vivid and also scarlet mouth and a low-pitched, accented voice." Films include *The Cold Deck* (1917), *The Narrow Trail* (1917), *We Can't Have Everything* (1918), *My Lady's Garter* (1920), *Doubling for Romeo* (1922), *The Girl of the Golden West* (1923), and *Up in Mabel's Room* (1926).

64. Evelyn Brent (1899–1975). The superb, icy cold heroine of *Underworld* (1927) and *The Last Command* (1928), Evelyn Brent began her film career in 1914 under her own name — Betty Riggs. She starred in thirteen films in England (1920–1922) and was on screen through 1950. Films include *The Pit* (1914), *The Lure of Heart's Desire* (1916; her first film as Evelyn Brent), *Raffles* (1917), *Love 'Em and Leave 'Em* (1926), *The Drag Net* (1928), and *Broadway* (1929).

65

65. Mary Brian (1908–). Mary Brian became a star and gained a long-term Paramount contract as a result of her performance as Wendy in *Peter Pan* (1924); she soon developed from a sweet, child-like ingénue to a dark-haired, mature beauty. One of the most reliable of Paramount stars and one of the best-loved actresses in the film industry. Films include *Beau Geste* (1926), *Brown of Harvard* (1926), *Running Wild* (1927), *Harold Teen* (1928), *The Virginian* (1929), and *The Front Page* (1931). Photograph by Cecil Beaton.

66

66. Gladys Brockwell (1894–1929). A superb and underrated character player equally at home in emotional or simpering roles, Gladys Brockwell is seen at her best in *The Hunchback of Notre Dame* (1923), *7th Heaven* (1927), and *Lights of New York* (1928). Films include *The Honor System* (1917), *The Devil's Wheel* (1920), *A Sister to Salome* (1920), *Oliver Twist* (1922), *Stella Maris* (1925), and *Long Pants* (1927).   **67. Betty Bronson** (1907–1971). The silent screen's *Peter Pan* (1924), Betty Bronson never really distinguished herself in any other film during her career, which continued on and off until her death in 1971. Films include *Are Parents People?* (1925), *Ben-Hur* (1926), *A Kiss for Cinderella* (1926), and *Sonny Boy* (1929).

67

69

68

69. Van Dyke Brooke (1859–1921). A former stage actor, Van Dyke Brooke was under contract to Vitagraph 1909-1916 as an actor, writer, and director. The company's co-founder, J. Stuart Blackton, described him as "genial" both on and off screen. Films include *My Old Dutch* (1911), *A Romance of Wall Street* (1912), *An Amateur Orphan* (1917), *The Moonshine Trail* (1919), *The Fortune Hunter* (1920), *The Passionate Pilgrim* (1921), and *The Son of Wallingford* (1921).

68. Clive Brook (1887–1974). A dignified, yet strong screen presence in American films from 1924, Clive Brook eclipsed his performances in silent films with his roles in *Cavalcade* (1932) and, best of all, *On Approval* (1945), which he also directed. Films include *Christine of the Hungry Heart* (1924), *Déclassée* (1925), *Three Faces East* (1926), *The Devil Dancer* (1927), and *Underworld* 1927).

71

70

71. Johnny Mack Brown (1904–1974). A former college football star who became an M-G-M contract player in 1927, Johnny Mack Brown did not become associated with Westerns until the talkies and his appearance in *Billy the Kid* (1930). Films include *The Fair Co-ed* (1927), *The Divine Woman* (1928), *A Woman of Affairs* (1928), and *Our Dancing Daughters* (1928).

70. Louise Brooks (1906–1985). A much vaunted performer who was little more than a featured player in American films, Louise Brooks looked beautiful and acted adequately. She was on screen from 1925 through 1938. Films include *It's the Old Army Game* (1926), *Rolled Stockings* (1927), *Beggars of Life* (1928), and *Overland Stage Raiders* (1938; her last film). Autobiography: *Lulu in Hollywood* (New York: Alfred A. Knopf, 1982).

72

73

72. Kate Bruce (1858–1946). Kate Bruce was a D. W. Griffith character actress who specialized in kindly, yet firm mother roles from 1909 into the twenties. She was most memorable as the gentle Mrs. Bartlett in *Way Down East* (1920); Lillian Gish took care of her in later years. Films include *The Country Doctor* (1909), *Judith of Bethulia* (1913), *Hearts of the World* (1918), *Orphans of the Storm* (1921), *The White Rose* (1923), and *A Bowery Cinderella* (1927).   **73. John Bunny** (1863–1915). John Bunny was the first major screen comedian and acted for the Vitagraph Company from 1910–1915; he was fat, jolly, and based on his extant films, not very funny. He was usually cast opposite thin and spinsterish Flora Finch, who apparently disliked him as much as did everyone else at the studio. Films include *Vanity Fair* (1911), *Cure for Pokeritus* (1912), *The Troublesome Stepdaughters* (1912), *Pickwick Papers* (1913), *When the Press Speaks* (1913), and *Pigs Is Pigs* (1914).

74

75

74. Billie Burke (1885–1970). Billie Burke was
a petite star of stage and screen, married to Florenz
Ziegfeld, and made her biggest and lasting impact as
Glinda, the Good Witch, in *The Wizard of Oz* (1939).
Films include *Peggy* (1916; her first film), *The Mysterious
Miss Terry* (1917), *Pursuit of Polly* (1918), *Good Gracious,
Annabelle* (1919), *The Frisky Mrs. Johnson* (1920), and
The Education of Elizabeth (1921). Autobiography: *With a
Feather on My Nose* (New York: Appleton-Century-
Crofts, 1949) and *With Powder on My Nose* (New York:
Coward-McCann, 1959).

75. Edmund/Edward Burns (1892–1980). A tall,
broad-shouldered actor with a good physique,
Edmund/Edward Burns began his screen career at Fox
after 3 ½ years of selling Kellogg's Corn Flakes. He
worked well opposite Valeska Suratt, Kitty Gordon,
Elsie Ferguson, Olga Petrova, and others. Films
include *Wild and Woolly* (1917), *Male and Female* (1919),
The Virgin of Stamboul (1920), *Abraham Lincoln* (1924),
The Million Dollar Handicap (1925), *Sunny Side Up*
(1926), and *The Shamrock and the Rose* (1927).

76

76. Neal Burns (1890–1969). A Christie comedy star of the 'teens and twenties, Neal Burns enjoyed some stage success and generally portrayed down-to- earth types with no particular comedic characteristics. Films include *Mary's Ankle* (1920), *That Son of a Sheik* (1922), *Court Plaster* (1924), and *Soup to Nuts* (1925).

77

78

77. Mae Busch (1897–1946). A statuesque silent star who began her career with Mack Sennett in the mid-'teens (she supposedly broke up Sennett's proposed marriage to actress Mabel Normand), Mae Busch ended up playing a stooge to the likes of Laurel and Hardy. She gained immortality thanks to Jackie Gleason's catchphrase, "and the ever-popular Mae Busch." Films include *Foolish Wives* (1922), *The Christian* (1923), *Bread* (1924), *The Unholy Three* (1925), *Fazil* (1928), *Doctor X* (1932), and *Bohemian Girl* (1936).

78. Pauline Bush (1886–1969). Leading lady with the American Film Company and Universal from 1911 through 1915, Pauline Bush usually co-starred with J. Warren Kerrigan. She married her director, Allan Dwan, in 1915 and retired, returning in 1924 for one film — *The Enemy Sex*. Films include *The Poisoned Flume* (1911), *Richelieu* (1914), *Her Escape* (1914), and *The Struggle* (1915).

79. Francis X. Bushman (1885–1966). In 1914, Francis X. Bushman, with his classic profile, was considered the most popular actor on the screen; by the late 'teens, his career was failing, but a featured role in *Ben-Hur* (1926) brought him back. He continued acting in minor roles until his death in 1966. Films include *Under Royal Patronage* (1914), *Romeo and Juliet* (1916), and *Red, White and Blue Blood* (1917). **80. David Butler** (1895–1979). A director of lightweight, popular fare, David Butler began his career as an extra in *The Birth of a Nation* (1915), graduating to leading man before turning to directing in 1927. Films include *The Greatest Thing in Life* (1918), *The County Fair* (1920), *The Sky Pilot* (1921), *His Majesty, Bunker Bean* (1925), *The Plastic Age* (1926), and *7th Heaven* (1927). **81. Alice Calhoun** (1900–1966). A featured actress of the twenties who became a star at Vitagraph from 1920 through 1925, Alice Calhoun was active through the early thirties. Films include *Everybody's Business* (1919), *Captain Swift* (1920), *The Little Minister* (1922), *Makers of Men* (1923), *Between Friends* (1924), *Pampered Youth* (1925), and *Savage Passions* (1927).

80

79

81

83

82

82. Catherine Calvert (1890–1971). Dramatic actress on screen from 1917 through 1922; married playwright Paul Armstrong. Films include *Behind the Mask* (1917), *Out of the Night* (1918), *Fires of Faith* (1919), *Dead Men Tell No Tales* (1920), *The Heart of Maryland* (1921), and *That Woman* (1922).

83. Yakima Canutt (1895–1986). A legendary stuntman active through 1976, Yakima Canutt's silent film work was minimal; he was responsible for classic stuntwork in *Stagecoach* (1939), stunt direction in *Ben-Hur* (1959), and received an Honorary Academy Award in 1966. Films include *The Heart of a Texan* (1922), *The Forbidden Range* (1923), *Ridin' Mad* (1924), *Scar Hanan* (1925), and *The Devil Horse* (1926). Autobiography: *Stunt Man* (New York: Walker, 1979).

84

85

86

87

84. June Caprice (1899–1936). A Fox star of the mid-'teens, June Caprice was described by a contemporary writer as "a wee bit of fluffy, golden-haired kiddie, with wide, blue eyes." Films include *Caprice of the Mountains* (1916), *A Modern Cinderella* (1917), *Oh, Boy!* (1919), *The Love Cheat* (1919), and *A Damsel in Distress* (1920). **85. Arthur Edmund Carewe** (1881–1940). Arthur Edmund Carewe was an actor whose looks always seemed best suited to the horror genre, as he proved in the twenties with roles in *The Phantom of the Opera* (1925) and *The Cat and the Canary* (1927), and later in sound with *Doctor X* (1932) and *The Mystery of the Wax Museum* (1933). Films include *The World and Its Women* (1919), *Daddy* (1923), *Sandra* (1924), *The Silent Lover* (1926), and *The Claw* (1927). **86. Ora Carewe** (1893–1955). After the commencement of her career

with Fine Arts in 1915, Ora Carewe switched to comedy with Mack Sennett in 1916. She later returned to more serious roles. Films include *The Martyrs of the Alamo* (1915), *Too Many Millions* (1918), *Blind Youth* (1920), *Ladyfingers* (1921), *Sherlock Brown* (1922), *The Torrent* (1924), and *Cold Fury* (1925; her last film). **87. Harry Carey** (1878–1947). Harry Carey entered films with D. W. Griffith at Biograph in 1909, but he is best known for the silent Westerns in which he starred under John Ford's direction. With the coming of sound, Carey became a fine supporting actor. Films include *The Musketeers of Pig Alley* (1912), *Straight Shooting* (1917), *The Outcasts of Poker Flats* (1919), *Desperate Trails* (1921), *Crashin' Thru* (1923), *The Night Hawk* (1924), and *Slide, Kelly, Slide* (1927).

88

89

90

88. Jewel Carmen (1897–). A beautiful, blonde actress who may be seen at her best in *A Tale of Two Cities* (1917), Jewel Carmen began her career in *Intolerance* (1916) and later became Douglas Fairbanks' leading lady. She retired from films in 1921 but returned in 1926 to star in *The Bat*, directed by her husband, Roland West. Films include *The Half Breed* (1916), *Flirting with Fate* (1916), *Les Misérables* (1917), *The Kingdom of Love* (1918), and *Nobody* (1921).   **89. Tullio Carminati** (1894–1971). A leading man in Italian (from 1912) and American (from 1926) silent films, Tullio Carminati was more closely associated with talkies. Films include *The Bat* (1926; his first U.S. film), *The Duchess of Buffalo* (1926), *Stage Madness* (1927), *Honeymoon Hats* (1927), and *Three Sinners* (1928). He appears in this photograph with actress Florence Vidor.   **90. Sue Carol** (1907–1981). One of the flapper stars of the late twenties, Sue Carol is probably better known today as the wife of Alan Ladd. Films include *Slaves of Beauty* (1927), *The Cohens and Kellys in Paris* (1928), *Walking Back* (1928), and *The Exalted Flapper* (1929).

91

91. Mary Carr (1874–1973). Noted for her "mother" roles, particularly in *Over the Hill to the Poorhouse* (1920), Mary Carr could arouse sympathy from an audience without evidencing that she could really act. Films include *Souls in Bondage* (1916), *The Barrier* (1917), *Mrs. Wiggs of the Cabbage Patch* (1919), *Broadway Broke* (1923), *Damaged Hearts* (1924), *Drusilla with a Million* (1925), and *The Show Girl* (1927).

92

93

94

92. Kenneth Casey (1899–1965). A child actor billed as "The Vitagraph Boy" and on screen from 1909, Kenneth Casey later became a songwriter. Films include *Chew Chew Land* (1910), *Ransomed, or A Prisoner of War* (1910), *A Little Lad in Dixie* (1911), *The Black Wall* (1912), and *When Bobby Forgot* (1913).   **93. Dolores Cassinelli** (–). Somewhat pretentious both on and off screen, Italian-born Dolores Cassinelli began her U. S. career with Essanay in the mid-'teens; she was also active on the concert and operatic stages. Films include *Zongar* (1918), *The Virtuous Model* (1919), *Tarnished Reputations* (1920), *Forever* (1921), *Columbus* (1923), and *The Midnight Girl* (1925).

94.   Helene Chadwick (1898–1940). A Goldwyn star of the late 'teens and early twenties whom *Motion Picture Classic* (January 1920) colored green and gold: "green, soft and cool for her shimmering school-girlishness — and gold for the dash of sophistication and wise knowing she possesses." Films include *Dangerous Curve Ahead* (1921), *The Sin Flood* (1922), *Reno* (1923), *Why Men Leave Home* (1924), *Dancing Days* (1926), and *Stolen Pleasures* (1927).

F 206-50

95

95. Irene Castle (1893–1969). With her husband, Vernon, Irene Castle was one of the most popular dancers of her generation and also a successful screen star. Fred Astaire and Ginger Rogers portrayed the couple in the 1939 RKO feature *The Story of Vernon and Irene Castle*. Films include *The Whirl of Life* (1915), *Patria* (1916), *The Mark of Cain* (1917), *The Girl from Bohemia* (1918), *The Common Cause* (1919), *The Amateur Wife* (1920), *French Heels* (1922), and *Broadway After Dark* (1924). Autobiography: *Castles in the Air* (Garden City, NY: Doubleday, 1958).

97

96. Lon Chaney (1883–1930). Lon Chaney was rightly dubbed "The Man of a Thousand Faces." He entered films in 1913, but will always be associated with the series of semi-horror features in which he starred for M-G-M in the twenties. Films include *The Miracle Man* (1919), *Treasure Island* (1920), *The Penalty* (1920), *Oliver Twist* (1922), *The Hunchback of Notre Dame* (1923), *The Unholy Three* (1925), *The Phantom of the Opera* (1925), *Mr. Wu* (1927), and *The Unholy Three* (1930; his last film).

97. Charles Chaplin (1889–1977). Charlie Chaplin was a complex individual who mingled politics with comedy in his later films only with moderate success. An English Music Hall comedian, Chaplin made his screen debut in 1914, introducing the "Tramp" character with whom he became immortal in *Kid Auto Races at Venice* (1914). Films include *Easy Street* (1917), *The Immigrant* (1917), *Shoulder Arms* (1918), *The Kid* (1921), *The Gold Rush* (1925), *The Circus* (1928), *Modern Times* (1936), *The Great Dictator* (1940), *Monsieur Verdoux* (1947), and *Limelight* (1952). Autobiography: *My Autobiography* (New York: Simon and Schuster, 1964).

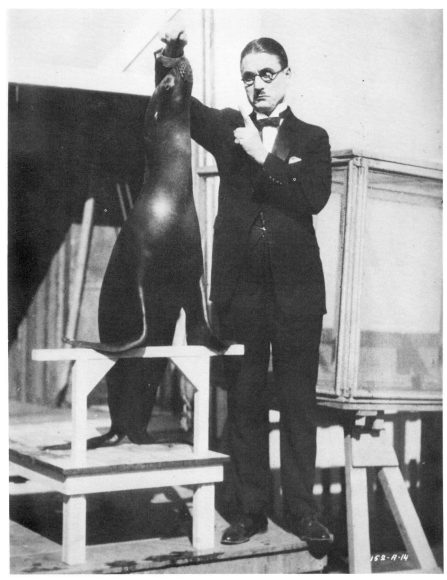

98

98. Sydney Chaplin (1885–1965). An older brother of Charlie of whom *Close Up* (February 1928) wrote: "At his most slapstick moments [he] does seem to have an individual and tragic quality that because of its restraint (almost repression) reaches a high point of art." Films include *A Submarine Pirate* (1915), *A Dog's Life* (1918), *The Pilgrim* (1923), *Charley's Aunt* (1925), *The Man on the Box* (1925), and *The Better 'Ole* (1926).

99. Mary Charleson (1890–1961). Following her debut with Selig, Mary Charleson became a Vitagraph leading lady and married actor Henry B. Walthall with whom she co-starred in later Essanay films. Films include *Mr. Barnes of New York* (1914), *The Road to Strife* (1915), *The Man Who Couldn't Kill Conscience* (1915), *Passers-By* (1916), *His Robe of Honor* (1918), and *Human Stuff* (1920).   **100. Charlie Chase** (1893–1940). Charlie Chase's comedy success lay in his looking like a harrassed middle-class businessman or husband when most comedians looked eccentric. He was on screen from 1914 until his death. Most historians consider his best work to be the almost 50 shorts he made for Leo McCarey between 1924 and 1926. Films include *Tillie's Punctured Romance* (1914), *Love, Loot and Crash* (1915), *Her Torpedoed Love* (1917), *All Wet* (1924), *What Price Goofy?* (1925), *Crazy Like a Fox* (1926), *Call of the Cuckoos* (1927), and *Movie Night* (1929).

99

100

101

102

101. Jack J. Clark (1876–1947). A Kalem leading man from 1910, Jack J. Clark became a member of the Gene Gauntier Feature Players in 1913 (where he was also a director). He then moved with his wife, Gene Gauntier (divorced in 1918), to Universal as a director and her leading man. Films include *Rory O'More* (1911), *The Colleen Bawn* (1911), *Poacher's Pardon* (1912), *Captured by Bedouins* (1912), *From the Manger to the Cross* (1912), *The Last of the Mafia* (1915), and *Audrey* (1916).

102. Marguerite Clark (1887–1940). The only major and legitimate rival to Mary Pickford, Marguerite Clark made 39 features, all but one of them under contract to Paramount, between 1914 and 1920. She is fondly remembered by those privileged enough to have seen her on stage (from 1899) or screen. Films include *Wildflower* (1914; her first film), *Snow White* (1916), *Prunella* (1918), *Uncle Tom's Cabin* (1918), and *Scrambled Wives* (1921; her last film).

103

103. Ethel Clayton (1883–1966). A contemporary writer commented, "The histrionic ability of Ethel Clayton was best represented in leading woman types exhibiting a quiet repression or silent suffering of a person in reversed circumstances." Her career lasted from 1910 through the late thirties, and included comedy as well as "silent suffering." Films include *The Lion and the Mouse* (1914), *The Great Divide* (1915), *Maggie Pepper* (1919), *A Sporting Chance* (1919), *Crooked Streets* (1920), *If I Were Queen* (1922), *Lightnin'* (1925), and *Mother Machree* (1928).   **104. Marguerite Clayton** (1891–1968). An Essanay leading lady from 1912–1917 who often played opposite "Broncho Billy" Anderson. Films include *The Birthmark* (1915) *The Prince of Graustark* (1916), *The Dream Doll* (1917), *Hit-the-Trail Holliday* (1918), *The New Moon* (1919), *Inside the Cup* (1921), *What Love Will Do* (1923), and *Twin Flappers* (1927).

104

105

106

105. Charles Clary (1873–1931). An actor who entered films with Selig in 1910 after a lengthy stage career: "I found free auto-rides, free luncheons on location and congenial people to act with," he told *Motion Picture* (June 1919). Films include *Two Orphans* (1911), *The Coming of Columbus* (1912), *The Adventures of Kathlyn* (1913), *Joan the Woman* (1917), *A Connecticut Yankee at King Arthur's Court* (1921), and *Beverly of Graustark* (1926). **106. Hal C. Clements** (–). A Kalem actor and director in the early 'teens who ended his career in the same decade as a featured player. Films include *The Rival Engineer* (1912), *A Treacherous Shot* (1913), *The Man Who Could Not Lose* (1914), *The Unknown* (1915), *Miss Jackie of the Army* (1917), and *Other Men's Wives* (1919). **107. Kathleen Clifford** (1894–1963). A male impersonator in vaudeville billed as "The Smartest Chap in Town," Kathleen Clifford enjoyed a film career as a very feminine star. Films include *Who Is Number One?* (1917), *Cold Steel* (1921), *Kick In* (1922), *Richard, The Lion-Hearted* (1923), *No More Woman* (1924), and *Sporting Life* (1925).

107

108. Ruth Clifford (1900–). A major Universal dramatic star of the late 'teens, Ruth Clifford later became one of the better known members of John Ford's stock company. Films include *The Savage* (1917), *The Desire of the Moth* (1917), *Fires of Youth* (1918), *The Kaiser, the Beast of Berlin* (1918), *The Cabaret Girl* (1919), *Ponjola* (1923), and *Abraham Lincoln* (1924). **109. William Collier, Jr.** (1902–1987). An attractive leading man from the late 'teens onwards and son of a well-known stage actor, William Collier, Jr., was often referred to as "Buster" after a stage role he played with his father in *Never Say Die* (1913). Films include *The Heart of Maryland* (1921), *The Age of Desire* (1923), *The Lighthouse by the Sea* (1924), *The Reckless Sex* (1925), *The Wanderer* (1926), and *Backstage* (1927). He appears in this photograph with actress Virginia Brown Faire.

108

109

110

110. Ronald Colman (1891–1958). On screen in his native England from 1919, Ronald Colman came to the States in 1921 and quickly gained a reputation as an acceptable, yet somewhat passive, leading man whose love scenes appeared to embarrass him. Films include *The White Sister* (1923), *Stella Dallas* (1925), *Lady Windermere's Fan* (1925), *Beau Geste* (1926), *The Winning of Barbara Worth* (1926), and more than twenty-five sound features. He appears in this photograph with actress Vilma Bank welcoming Spanish chanteuse Raquel Meller (center) to the Goldwyn Studios.

111. Betty Compson (1897–1974). A busy and competent actress in silents and early talkies with more than 150 films to her credit, Betty Compson began her career as a leading lady in Christie Comedies in 1915. Films include *The Miracle Man* (1919), *The Little Minister* (1922), *Woman to Woman* (1923), *Beggar on Horseback* (1925), *The Pony Express* (1925), *The Docks of New York* (1928), *On With the Show* (1929), *The Great Gabbo* (1929), *The Spoilers* (1930), and *Here Comes Trouble* (1948; her last film).

112

113

112. Chester Conklin (1886–1971). A Mack Sennett comedian famous for his walrus moustache (which provided him with the nickname "Fish Face"), Chester Conklin was on screen from 1913 through the sixties. Films include *Tillie's Punctured Romance* (1914), *Love, Speed and Thrills* (1915), *Anna Christie* (1923), *Greed* (1925), *Behind the Front* (1926), *McFadden's Flats* (1927), and *Gentlemen Prefer Blondes* (1928).

113. Jackie Coogan (1914–1984). The best-known of all the silent child stars, Jackie Coogan came to fame with Chaplin in *The Kid* (1921) and consolidated that fame with *Oliver Twist* (1922). As a character actor in later years, he was usually far superior to the films in which he appeared. Films include *Skinner's Baby* (1917; his first film), *A Day's Pleasures* (1919), *Peck's Bad Boy* (1921), *Daddy* (1923), *A Boy of Flanders* (1924), and *Buttons* (1927).

114. Guy Coombs (1882-????). Entered films with Edison, but rose to prominence when he joined the Kalem Company in September, 1911; for much of the silent era, he was merely a featured player. Films include *The Octoroon* (1913), *The School for Scandal* (1914), *The Call of the Dance* (1915), *My Madonna* (1915), *Bab's Diary* (1917), *Loaded Dice* (1918), *The Wrong Woman* (1920), and *When Knighthood was in Flower* (1922). **115. Miriam Cooper** (1891-1976). Miriam Cooper entered films with D. W. Griffith in 1911; became a Kalem Company star (1912-1913); and gave memorable, modernistic performances in *The Birth of a Nation* (1915) and *Intolerance* (1916). She was later a Fox star, working under the direction of her husband, Raoul Walsh. Films include *A Blot on the 'Scutcheon* (1911; her first film), *Home, Sweet Home* (1914), *The Honor System* (1917), *Evangeline* (1919), and *Kindred of the Dust* (1922). Autobiography: *Dark Lady of the Silents* (New York: Bobbs-Merrill, 1973).

114

115

116

116. Virginia Lee Corbin (1910–1942). One of the cutest Fox child stars of the late 'teens, Virginia Lee Corbin was featured in a number of adaptations of well-known fairy tales. She performed adequately later as an adult in *Hands Up!* (1926). Films include *The Babes in the Woods* (1917), *Treasure Island* (1918), *The Forbidden Room* (1919), *The White Dove* (1920), *Enemies of Children* (1923), and *Wine of Youth* (1924).

117. Maria Corda (1902–). Star of only two U. S. silent features: *The Private Life of Helen of Troy* (1927) and *Love and the Devil* (1929), both directed by her husband, Alexander Korda, for whom she had earlier starred in six German features from 1923 through 1926. **118. Ricardo Cortez** (1899–1977). As his roles in *The Pony Express* (1925) and *The Sorrows of Satan* (1926) indicate, Ricardo Cortez deserves to be remembered as far more than a replacement for Rudolph Valentino. He was on screen from 1923 through 1940 and is the brother of celebrated cinematographer Stanley Cortez. Films include *The Spaniard* (1925), *The Swan* (1925), *The Torrent* (1926), *The Younger Generation* (1929), and *The Maltese Falcon* (1931).

117

118

119

119. Dolores (1905–1979) and **Helene Costello** (1903–1957). The daughters of actor Maurice Costello, both women began their film careers as children at Vitagraph circa 1911. They retired from the screen to pursue their educations and returned as stars in the early twenties. Dolores, the more prominent and the better actress of the two, married John Barrymore; but Helene has a special place in film history as the star of the first Vitaphone all-talking feature: *Lights of New York* (1928). Dolores ended her film career with a fine performance in Orson Welles' *The Magnificent Ambersons* (1942). Dolores' films include *The Sea Beast* (1926), *The Third Degree* (1927), *Old San Francisco* (1927), and *Glorious Betsy* (1928). Helene's films include *The Man on the Box* (1925), *Don Juan* (1926), and *The Heart of Maryland* (1927).   **120. Maurice Costello** (1877–1950). The first major star of the Vitagraph Company from 1907–1915, Maurice Costello was affectionately known to his fans as "Dimples." His screen career diminished in the twenties, and he played as an extra until his death. Films include *A Tale of Two Cities* (1911), *As You Like It* (1912), *The Crimson Stain Mystery* (1916), *Tower of Jewels* (1920), *Fog Bound* (1923), *Virtuous Liars* (1924), and *Camille* (1927).

120

121

122

121. Anne Cornwall (1897–1980). A former chorus girl, Anne Cornwall began her career as an ingénue at Universal. Films include *The Knife* (1918), *The World To Live In* (1919), *La La Lucille* (1920), *Her Gilded Cage* (1922), *Dulcy* (1923), *The Rainbow Trail* (1925), *Under Western Skies* (1926), and *College* (1927).

122. Joan Crawford (1904–1977). There was something light and gay about Joan Crawford in silent films and early talkies, an image that disappeared as the actress began to take herself too seriously. Films include *Tramp, Tramp, Tramp* (1926), *The Unknown* (1927), *Our Dancing Daughters* (1928), *Our Modern Maidens* (1929), and sound films in the next four decades. Autobiography: *A Portrait of Joan* (Garden City, NY: Doubleday, 1962) and *My Way of Life* (New York: Simon and Schuster, 1971).

123

124

125

123. Donald Crisp (1882–1974). Memorable as Lillian Gish's brutal father in *Broken Blossoms* (1919), Donald Crisp began his career with D. W. Griffith in 1909. He turned to directing in the twenties but returned to acting with the coming of sound. Films include *The Battle* (1911), *The Escape* (1914), *The Birth of a Nation* (1915), and *Believe Me Xantippe* (1918). In this picture he looks down on actor Bryant Washburn.

124. Grace Cunard (1893–1967). With Francis Ford, Grace Cunard was a top Universal serial star of the 'teens who tried her hand, unsuccessfully, at directing. In films from 1912, she ended her career as a "bit" player. Films include *Lucille Love, Girl of Mystery* (1914 serial), *The Broken Coin* (1915 serial), *Society's Driftwood* (1917), *Elmo the Mighty* (1919 serial), and *The Girl in the Taxi* (1921).

125. Dorothy Dalton (1893–1972). A strikingly unusual face plus a fine dramatic talent, but the films in which Dorothy Dalton usually starred, from 1914 through 1924, seldom did her justice with the honorable exception of *Moran of the Lady Letty* (1922). Films include *D'Artagnan* (1916), *Flame of the Yukon* (1917), *Vive la France* (1918), and *The Moral Sinner* (1924; her last film).

126

126. Viola Dana (1898–1987). Viola Dana made her screen debut with her sister, Shirley Mason, in Edison's *A Christmas Carol* (1910), and she spent the next thirteen years as one of the cinema's busiest and most popular, winsome stars. She was under contract to Metro from 1916–1924; and between 1916 and 1918, she starred in more than a dozen features directed by her husband, John Collins. Films include *Molly, the Drummer Boy* (1914), *The Stoning* (1915), *Blue Jeans* (1917), *The Off-Shore Pirate* (1921), *Revelation* (1924), *Merton of the Movies* (1924), and *That Certain Thing* (1928).

128

127

127. Karl Dane (1886–1934). A Danish-born actor
whose accent and the coming of sound ended his career
and made him a suicide victim, Karl Dane was splendid
as the American doughboy "Slim" in *The Big Parade*
(1925) and in a series of comedy shorts with George K.
Arthur. Films include *La Bohème* (1926), *The Scarlet
Letter* (1926), *Bardelys the Magnificent* (1926), and *The
Red Mill* (1927).   **128. Bebe Daniels** (1901–1971). A
top Hollywood star who, with her husband, Ben Lyon,
became one of Britain's best-loved radio personalities.
She began her screen career with Selig and was Harold
Lloyd's leading lady from 1915 through 1919 before
becoming a Paramount contract star from 1919 through
1928. Films include *Male and Female* (1919), *Sick Abed*
(1920), *The Affairs of Anatol* (1921), *Monsieur Beaucaire*
(1924), *Volcano* (1926), *Rio Rita* (1929), *42nd Street*
(1933), and *The Lyons in Paris* (1956; her last film).
Autobiography: *Life with the Lyons* (London: Odhams,
1953).

129

130

129. Roy D'Arcy (1894–1969). Wonderfully convincing in slimy and lecherous roles, Roy D'Arcy was at his best under Erich von Stroheim's direction in *The Merry Widow* (1925). Films include *Graustark* (1925), *La Bohème (1926), Bardelys the Magnificent* (1926), *The Temptress* (1926), *Adam and Evil* (1927), and *The Actress* (1928).

130. Grace Darmond (1898–1963). Usually featured in "B" films and serials such as *The Shielding Shadow* (1916) and *A Dangerous Adventure* (1922), Grace Darmond was also the star of the first Technicolor feature, *The Gulf Between* (1918). Films include *A Black Sheep* (1915), *A Diplomatic Mission* (1918), *So Long Letty* (1920), *The Beautiful Gambler* (1921), *Alimony* (1924), *The Night Patrol* (1926), and *Wages of Conscience* (1927).

131

131. Dorothy Davenport (1895–1977). An actress, director, producer, and writer from the well-known theatrical family, Dorothy Davenport billed herself as Mrs. Wallace Reid following the 1923 death of her husband. Films include *A Troublesome Baby* (1910), *Mr. Grex of Monte Carlo* (1915), *Black Friday* (1916), *Treason* (1917), *The Fighting Chance* (1920), *The Test* (1922), and *Human Wreckage* (1923).

132

132. Marion Davies (1897–1961). If she were not remembered as William Randolph Hearst's mistress, Marion Davies might well be recalled as one of the silent screen's finest comediennes. On screen from 1917 through 1937, her career was overshadowed by that of Hearst, and an unfair comparison between her and Orson Welles' Susan Alexander in *Citizen Kane* (1941) did not help. Films include *Runaway Romany* (1917; her first film), *When Knighthood Was in Flower* (1922), *Little Old New York* (1923), *Janice Meredith* (1924), *Quality Street* (1927), *The Patsy* (1928), and *Show People* (1928). Autobiography: *The Times We Had* (Indianapolis: Bobbs-Merrill, 1975).

133

134

133. Yola D'Avril (1907–1984). After her selection for appearance in *The Dressmaker from Paris* (1925) by designer Jean Patou, Yola D'Avril was signed to a Paramount contract. For most of her career, however, roles were small and inconsequential. Films include *Orchids and Ermine* (1927), *Smile, Brother, Smile* (1927), *American Beauty* (1927), *The Noose* (1928), and *Lady Be Good* (1928).

134. Marjorie Daw (1902–). "The Girl with the Nursery Rhyme Name" was discovered by Geraldine Farrar and came to stardom as Douglas Fairbanks' leading lady in seven films between 1918 and 1919. Films include *Joan the Woman* (1916), *Rebecca of Sunnybrook Farm* (1917), *A Modern Musketeer* (1918), *His Majesty the American* (1919), *The River's End* (1920), *Dinty* (1920), *A Fool There Was* (1922), *Revelation* (1924), and *Topsy and Eva* (1927).

135

136

135. Hazel Dawn (1891–1988). Known as "The Pink Lady" after the 1911 stage musical in which she starred, Hazel Dawn enjoyed a brief film career in the 'teens with Famous Players. Films include *One of Our Girls* (1914), *The Heart of Jennifer* (1915), *My Lady Incog.* (1916), and *The Lone Wolf* (1917).

136. Marceline Day (1909–). *Photoplay* magazine described this actress, who was a leading lady to everyone at M-G-M from Lon Chaney to Buster Keaton, as "a slender, soulful type." Films include *The White Outlaw* (1925), *The Boy Friend* (1926), *The Beloved Rogue* (1927), *Rookies* (1927), and *The Cameraman* (1928).

137

138

137. Priscilla Dean (1896–1988). Priscilla Dean began her career as a leading lady in 'teens comedies but quickly graduated to Universal dramas to which she added a statuesque presence. Films include *The Wildcat of Paris* (1918), *The Virgin of Stamboul* (1920), *Outside the Law* (1921), *Under Two Flags* (1922), *White Tiger* (1923), *West of Broadway* (1926), and *Jewels of Desire* (1927).

138. Sam de Grasse (1875–1953). A competent and busy character actor who began his screen career with D. W. Griffith. Films include *The Martyrs of the Alamo* (1915), *Intolerance* (1916), *Wild and Woolly* (1917), *Blind Husbands* (1919), *The Devil's Passkey* (1920), *Robin Hood* (1922), *The Black Pirate* (1926), *The King of Kings* (1927), and *Our Dancing Daughters* (1928).

139

140

141

139. Mr. (1886–1977) and **Mrs. Carter (Flora) De Haven** (1883–1950). Mr. and Mrs. De Haven were exponents of light comedy in the style of Mr. and Mrs. Sidney Drew, but they were not as skillful. De Haven later became an assistant director with credits including *Modern Times* (1936). Films include *The College Orphan* (1915), *The Wrong Door* (1916), *Honey-Mooning* (1919), *Twin Beds* (1920), *The Girl in the Taxi* (1921), *My Lady Friends* (1921), and *Marry the Poor Girl* (1921). **140. Marguerite De La Motte** (1902–1950). In films from the late 'teens, Marguerite De La Motte became a star when Douglas Fairbanks selected her as his leading lady for *The Mark of Zorro* (1920). She was, at one time, married to actor John Bowers. Films include *A Sagebrush Hamlet* (1919), *Trumpet Island* (1920), *The Nut* (1921), *Shadows* (1922), *The Clean Heart* (1924), *The Unknown Soldier* (1926), and *The Iron Mask* (1929).

141. Philippe De Lacey (1917–). Every other child in major features of the twenties seemed to be played by Philippe De Lacey, an actor whose career ended in the thirties. As an adult, he became an advertising executive. He was particularly cute as "Michael" in *Peter Pan* (1924). Films include *Rosita* (1923), *Beau Geste* (1926), *Don Juan* (1926), *The Student Prince in Old Heidelberg* (1927), *Mother Machree* (1928), and *Four Devils* (1929).

142

143

142. Dolores Del Rio (1905–1983). A dark-haired, Mexican beauty who made her screen debut in *Joanna* (1925), Dolores Del Rio was without question one of the most attractive of all screen stars, although her acting was not particularly inspiring. Films include *What Price Glory* (1926), *Loves of Carmen* (1927), *The Red Dance* (1928), and *Ramona* (1928).   **143. Carol Dempster** (1902–). D. W. Griffith discovered Carol Dempster and tried to mold her into another Lillian Gish. He failed, despite a valiant effort by both director and star in *Isn't Life Wonderful* (1924) and *The Sorrows of Satan* (1926). Dempster was an unconventional beauty who seemed to keep her distance from the roles she was playing. Films include *Dream Street* (1921), *Sherlock Holmes* (1922), *The White Rose* (1923), *America* (1924), and *Sally of the Sawdust* (1925).   **144. Reginald Denny** (1891–1967). An English-born actor on stage from 1908 and in American films from 1919, Reginald Denny gained stardom in "The Leather Pushers" series (1922–1924). He was regarded as a superior light comedian. Films include *Bringing Up Betty* (1919; his

first American film), *59 East* (1920), *Sherlock Holmes* (1922), *Sporting Youth* (1924), *California Straight Ahead* (1925), and *Skinner's Dress Suit* (1926).   **145. Rubye de Remer** (????–1984). A Ziegfeld *Follies* beauty, Rubye de Remer was very lovely but incapable of any expression. She quit the screen to marry millionarie Ben Throop. Films include *Enlighten Thy Daughter* (1917), *For Freedom* (1918), *A Fool and His Money* (1920), *Luxury* (1921), *Unconquered Woman* (1922), and *The Glimpses of the Moon* (1923). She appears in this photograph with her husband, Ben Throop.   **146. William Desmond** (1878–1949). A husky leading man who graduated from melodramas to action pictures to Westerns, William Desmond was active in films into the forties. Films include *Peer Gynt* (1915), *Peggy* (1916), *Wild Life* (1918), *Twin Beds* (1920), *Women Men Love* (1921), *Night Life in Hollywood* (1922), *The Extra Girl* (1923), *The Measure of a Man* (1924), *Blood and Steel* (1925), and *Red Clay* (1927). He appears in this photograph with actress Mildred Harris.

144

145

146

148

147

147. Dorothy Devore (1899–1976). One of the best of the Christie Comedy female stars of the late 'teens and early twenties, Dorothy Devore was, perhaps, a little too charming to make it into the major leagues of screen comediennes. Films include *Know Thy Wife* (1918), *Forty-Five Minutes from Broadway* (1920), *Hold Your Breath* (1924), *His Majesty, Bunker Bean* (1925), and *The Wrong Mr. Wright* (1927).   **148. Elliot Dexter** (1870–1941). A stage juvenile who became Cecil B. DeMille's favorite leading man of the 'teens, Elliott Dexter was on screen from 1915 through 1926; married actress Marie Doro. Films include *Daphne and the Pirate* (1916), *The Heart of Nora Flynn* (1916), *Diplomacy* (1916), *A Romance of the Redwoods* (1917), *The Whispering Chorus* (1917), *Don't Change Your Husband* (1918), *The Squaw Man* (1918), *Something to Think About* (1920), *The Affairs of Anatol* (1921), *Adam's Rib* (1923), and *Stella Maris* (1925).

149

150

149. Richard Dix (1893–1949). A stolid, masculine leading man (jokingly referred to as "The Jaw"), Richard Dix was at his best as a "Native American Indian" in *The Vanishing American* (1925) and *Redskin* (1929), and at his worst in *Cimarron* (1931). When not cast as an Indian during his 1923–1929 starring contract with Paramount, he played clean-cut, all-Americans. Films include *The Glorious Fool* (1922), *The Christian* (1923), *The Ten Commandments* (1923), *Seven Keys to Baldpate* (1929), and *The Lost Squadron* (1932).   **150. Marie Doro** (1882–1956). Marie Doro was an important stage actress who enjoyed a brief screen career in the 'teens under contract to Famous Players. Films include *The Morals of Marcus* (1915), *Oliver Twist* (1916), *Diplomacy* (1916), *The Wood Nymph* (1916), and *Castles for Two* (1917).

151

152

151. Billie Dove (1901–). A Ziegfeld *Follies* beauty, Billie Dove entered films in 1921 and was as noted for her romance with Howard Hughes as for her acting ability. Films include *Polly of the Follies* (1922), *Wanderer of the Wasteland* (1924), *The Black Pirate* (1926), *Kid Boots* (1926), *The Sensation Seekers* (1927), and *Blondie of the Follies* (1933; her last film).

152. Louise Dresser (1878–1965). A slightly plump, important stage actress, Louise Dresser was memorable in silent films as *The Goose Woman* (1925) and as Catherine the Great in *The Eagle* (1925). Later, she was featured as the Russian Empress in *The Scarlet Empress* (1934). Films include *Burning Sands* (1922), *Ruggles of Red Gap* (1923), *Percy* (1925), *The Third Degree* (1926), *Mr. Wu* (1927), and *The Garden of Eden* (1928).

153. Marie Dressler (1869–1934). A major vaudeville and comedy star, Marie Dressler played Tillie in three 'teens features: *Tillie's Punctured Romance* (1914), *Tillie's Tomato Surprise* (1915), and *Tillie Wakes Up* (1916). She returned to films again in the late twenties as her stage career declined. Films include *The Callahans and the Murphys* (1927), *The Patsy* (1928), and *The Divine Lady* (1929). Autobiography: *The Life Story of an Ugly Duckling* (New York: Robert M. McBride, 1924) and *My Own Story* (Boston: Little, Brown, 1934).

153

154

154. Mr. (1864–1919) and **Mrs. Sidney Drew**
(1890–1925). The Drews were specialists from 1914
onwards in what Drew described as "sentimental
human comedy," first at Vitagraph and then at Metro.
Mrs. Drew (Lucille McVey) also directed, and Mr.
Drew was a great light comedian in his own right at
Vitagraph, most notably in *A Florida Enchantment*
(1914). Films include *Playing Dead* (1915), *His Wife's
Mother* (1916), *The Pest* (1917), *The Professional Patient*
(1917), and *Pay Day* (1918).   **155. Dorothy Dunbar**
(–). Minor actress of the twenties. Films include *The
Flaming Crisis* (1924), *The Amateur Gentleman* (1926),
Breed of the Sea (1926), and *What Price Love* (1927).

155

WILLIAM DUNCAN
TRADE S MARK
Selig Players

156

156. William Duncan (1879–1961). Rugged leading man who began his film career at Selig in 1912, moved to Vitagraph in 1916, and ended his career at Universal in the twenties; the type of an actor of whom it might be said that he acted with his chest. Films include *The Chalice of Courage* (1915), *God's Country and the Woman* (1916), *Aladdin from Broadway* (1917), *Where Men Are Men* (1921), *The Silent Vow* (1922), and *Smashing Barriers* (1923).   **157. Miss Du Pont** (1894–1973). Patricia Du Pont, known professionally as Miss Du Pont, began her screen career as Margaret Armstrong; she was described as "the quintessence of what a woman should be to whom all things have come easily, richly," and was seen at her best in *Foolish Wives* (1922). Films include *Bonnie May* (1920), *Brass* (1923), *So This Is Marriage* (1924), and *Mantrap* (1926).

157

158

158. Dorothy Dwan (1907–). She began her screen
career as an extra at Universal and later married Larry
Semon, opposite whom she played in his last features.
Films include *The Silent Vow* (1922), *The Wizard of Oz*
(1925), *The Perfect Clown* (1925), *The Great K & A Train
Robbery* (1926), and *McFadden's Flats* (1927).   **159.
Jeanne Eagels** (1894–1929). She was a tragic dramatic
actress of the stage whose two sound features in
1929 — *The Letter* and *Jealousy* — and occasional silent
features never did her justice. Films include *The World
and the Woman* (1916), *Fires of Youth* (1917), and *Man,
Woman and Sin* (1927).

159

160

161

160. Edward Earle (1882–1972). Claimed to be Mary Pickford's first leading man (on stage in Canada); entered films with Edison and later became typecast as an all-American in films for Metro and Vitaraph. Films include *The Great Divide* (1915), *The Barrier* (1917), *Blind Love* (1920), *East Lynne* (1921), *The Man Who Played God* (1922), *The Dangerous Flirt* (1924), *Irene* (1926), and *The Wind* (1928).

161. Helen Jerome Eddy (1897–). Helen Jerome Eddy was not exactly pretty, but she had a simple and direct appeal and was the perfect "hometown girl" in films of the late 'teens and twenties. Films include *Turn in the Road* (1919), *The Tong Man* (1919), *The County Fair* (1920), *Pollyanna* (1920), *The Country Kid* (1922), *Camille* (1927), and *15 Washington Square* (1928).

162

163

163. Marie Eline (1902–1981). Billed as "The Thanhouser Kidlet" from 1909 through 1914, Marie Eline was one of the most popular of the company's players, although few knew her real name. Films include *Jane Eyre* (1910), *She* (1911 and 1912), *When The Studio Burned* (1913), *Coals of Fire* (1914), and *Uncle Tom's Cabin* (1914).

162. Robert Edeson (1868–1931). Robert Edeson was on screen from 1914, ending the silent era as a supporting star at the DeMille Studio. Films include *How Molly Malone Made Good* (1915), *The Light That Failed* (1916), *Eyes of Youth* (1919), *The Prisoner of Zenda* (1922), *The Spoilers* (1923), *Feet of Clay* (1924), *Braveheart* (1925), *The Volga Boatman* (1926), *Chicago* (1927), and *Walking Back* (1928).

164

165

165. Bessie Eyton (1890-????). A prominent Selig leading lady married to director Charles Eyton; she joined the company in 1911 after a screen debut with Pathé. Films include *In the Days of the Thundering Herd* (1914), *The Spoilers* (1914), *The Crisis* (1916), *The Heart of Texas Ryan* (1917), *The Still Alarm* (1918), *Cheap Kisses* (1924), and *The Girl of Gold* (1925).

164. Howard Estabrook (1884-1978). A major screenwriter — *Cimarron* (1931), *A Bill of Divorcement* (1932), *David Copperfield* (1935), etc. — who left a stage career to become a screen actor in the early 'teens. Films include *Officer 666* (1914), *The Four Feathers* (1915), *M'Liss* (1915), *The Mysteries of Myra* (1916), and *The Wild Girl* (1917).

166. Elinor Fair (1903–1957). A nondescript leading lady; at her best opposite husband William Boyd in *The Volga Boatman* (1926) and *The Yankee Clipper* (1927). Films include *The Miracle Man* (1919), *Kismet* (1920), *White Hands* (1922), *The Law Forbids* (1924), *Gold and the Girl* (1925), and *Jim the Conqueror* (1927). **167. Douglas Fairbanks** (1883–1939). Douglas Fairbanks was everything a male silent star should be: athletic, good-looking, dashing, and talented. He was also married to America's Sweetheart, Mary Pickford. A former major stage actor, Fairbanks exuded good humor in all of his films; as one writer said, "He was America's greatest exponent of the smile." Films include *The Lamb* (1915; his first film), *The Mark of Zorro* (1920), *The Three Musketeers* (1921), *Robin Hood* (1922), *The Thief of Bagdad* (1924), *The Black Pirate* (1926), *The Gaucho* (1928), *The Taming of the Shrew* (1929), and *The Private Life of Don Juan* (1934; his last film).

167

166

168

168. Virginia Brown Faire (1904–1980). The original screen Tinker Bell in *Peter Pan* (1924) and a charming, unpretentious actress, Virginia Brown Faire came to Hollywood after winning a 1919 fan magazine contest. Her career lasted through the mid-thirties. Films include *Without Benefit of Clergy* (1921), *Omar the Tentmaker* (1922), *Monte Cristo* (1922), *His People* (1925), *The Temptress* (1926), and *Tracked by the Police* (1927). She plays a dual role in this photograph.

169

170

169. Dustin Farnum (1874–1929). A prominent U. S. stage actor (from 1897), Dustin Farnum recreated some of his stage successes on screen — *The Virginian* (1914) and *Cameo Kirby* (1914) — and was the star of the original film version of *The Squaw Man* (1914). Films include *Soldiers of Fortune* (1914), *The Gentleman from Indiana* (1915), *David Garrick* (1916), *The Scarlet Pimpernel* (1917), *The Light of Western Skies* (1918), *The Corsican Brothers* (1920), *Oath-Bound* (1922), *The Buster* (1923), *My Man* (1924), and *The Flaming Frontier* (1926). **170. Franklyn Farnum** (1878–1961). Universal leading man of the 'teens who came to the company in 1916 and quickly became known for his "Douglas Fairbanks smile." Films include *Love Never Dies* (1916), *Anything Once* (1917), *The Empty Cab* (1918), *The Land of Jazz* (1920), *Texas* (1922), *It Happened Out West* (1923), and *Border Intrigue* (1925).

171

171. William Farnum (1876–1953). A major Fox star of the 'teens who specialized in costume drama, William Farnum began his career at Selig in 1914 as the original Roy Glennister in *The Spoilers*. Films include *The Sign of the Cross* (1914), *The Nigger* (1915), *Fighting Blood* (1916), *A Tale of Two Cities* (1917), *Les Misérables* (1918), *Drag Harlan* (1920), *If I Were King* (1920), *Moonshine Valley* (1922), and *The Man Who Fights Alone* (1924).   **172. Geraldine Farrar** (1882–1967). She was the only opera star to become a major silent star with fourteen films between 1915 and 1920 to her credit. Films include *Carmen* (1915; her first film), *Maria Rosa* (1916), *Joan the Woman* (1917), and *The World and Its Woman* (1919). Autobiography: *Autobiography of Geraldine Farrar: Such Sweet Compulsion* (New York: Greystone, 1938).   **173. Charles Farrell** (1901–). Charles Farrell was an insipid leading man (to Rin-Tin-Tin) in *Clash of the Wolves* (1925) who suddenly developed muscles and acting ability with *Old Ironsides* (1926); he and Janet Gaynor were the essence of cuteness in late silents and early talkies. Films include *7th Heaven* (1927), *Fazil* (1928), *Street Angel* (1928), *Sunnyside Up* (1929), and *Liliom* (1930).

172

173

174. George Fawcett (1860–1939). Expert at father roles, George Fawcett was featured in a number of D. W. Griffith productions of the 'teens and also in the director's *Lady of the Pavements* (1929). He was dubbed by *Photoplay* magazine as "the Grand Young Man of the Screen." Films include *The Majesty of the Law* (1915), *The Crisis* (1916), *Panthea* (1917), *Hearts of the World* (1918), *True Heart Susie* (1919), *Two Weeks* (1920), *Manslaughter* (1922), *Java Head* (1923), *The Circle* (1925), *Love* (1927), and *Tempest* (1928).   **175. Julia Faye** (1893–1966). A Cecil B. DeMille contract player from the 'teens through the fifties, Julia Faye was rumored to be one of his mistresses. Films include *Don Quixote* (1916), *The Squaw Man* (1918), *Male and Female* (1919), *The Life of the Party* (1920), *Manslaughter* (1922), *Adam's Rib* (1923), *The Road to Yesterday* (1925), and *The Yankee Clipper* (1927).   **176. Louise Fazenda** (1895–1962). A popular comedienne whose natural beauty was usually hidden by eccentric makeup, Louise Fazenda entered films with Universal in 1913 and became a star with Mack Sennett two years later. Films include *Down on the Farm* (1920), *Quincy Adams Sawyer* (1922), *Galloping Fish* (1924), *Déclassée* (1925), *The Bat* (1926), *The Red Mill* (1927), and *Heart to Heart* (1928).

175

174

176

MAUDE FEALY
THANHOUSER

177

APEDA
N.Y.

178

177. Maude Fealy (1883–1971). Maude Fealy was a prominent stage actress who played opposite Henry Irving and was in Thanhouser films from 1911 through 1914. She made occasional screen appearances through 1916, and in the thirties through the fifties. Films include *The Early Life of David Copperfield* (1911; her first film), *King René's Daughter* (1913), *Frou Frou* (1914), *Pamela Congreve* (1914), and *The Immortal Flame* (1916).

178. Elsie Ferguson (1883–1961). Known as the "Aristocrat of the Screen," Elsie Ferguson was a noted beauty of stage (from 1900) and screen, none of whose films has survived for evaluation. She made 22 features for Paramount between 1917 and 1922, and one talkie for First National. Films include *Barbary Sheep* (1917; her first film), *A Doll's House* (1918), *Forever* (1921), and *Scarlet Pages* (1930; her last film).

179

180

179. Helen Ferguson (1901–1977). Graduated from stenographer to featured player at Fox in the 'teens; later, an agent. Helen Ferguson is good as Diana Deacon in *Miss Lulu Bett* (1921). Films include *Fools for Love* (1917), *Life's Greatest Problems* (1919), *Just Pals* (1920), *Hungry Hearts* (1922), *Brass* (1923), and *The Isle of Hope* (1925). **Audrey Ferris**, see entry No. 423.   **180. Romaine Fielding** (1868–1927). A Lubin leading man of the early 'teens (1912–1915); *The Moving Picture World* called him "four in one" because he was an actor, author, director, and manager. Films include *The Battle of Gettysburg* (1914), *The Eagle's Nest* (1915), *Youth* (1917), *Woman's Man* (1921), and *Ten Modern Commandments* (1927).

181

182

181. W. C. Fields (1879–1946). A major vaudeville comedian whose films happily capture the routines that he made famous on stage; at his best in sound features. Films include *Pool Sharks* (1915; his first film), *Janice Meredith* (1924), *Sally of the Sawdust* (1925), *That Royle Girl* (1925), *It's the Old Army Game* (1926), *Running Wild* (1927), and *Tillie's Punctured Romance* (1928).

182. Margarita Fischer (1886–1975). On stage from the age of six, Margarita Fischer entered films in the mid-'teens (she dropped the "c" from her name during the First World War because it looked too Germanic). She married director Harry Pollard and often starred in his features. Films include *The Pearl of Paradise* (1916), *Miss Jackie of the Navy* (1917), *K-The Unknown* (1924), and *Uncle Tom's Cabin* (1927).

183. Bess Flowers (1898–1984). Bess Flowers appeared in literally hundreds of films through 1964 as a bit player or extra, and became known as "Hollywood's Best Dressed Extra." She also enjoyed a career as a featured player in silent films from 1922. Films include *A Woman of Paris* (1923), *Hollywood* (1923), *Glenister of the Mounted* (1926), *The Greater Glory* (1926), *Irene* (1926), and *Blondes by Choice* (1927).

184. Maurice "Lefty" Flynn (1893–1959). A somewhat ungainly leading man of the twenties, "Lefty" Flynn's biggest role was opposite his then-wife, Viola Dana, in *Open All Night* (1924). Films include *Children of the Night* (1921), *Omar the Tentmaker* (1922), *Salomy Jane* (1923), *High and Handsome* (1925), and *The College Boob* (1926). **185. Ralph Forbes** (1905–1951). Ralph Forbes was an innocuous leading man who began his screen career in his native England with films such as *Comin' Thro' the Rye* (1923). He enjoyed an American career from the mid-twenties through the forties; even in silent films, he always managed to look very English. Films include *Beau Geste* (1926), *Mr. Wu* (1927), *The Enemy* (1927), and *The Whip* (1928).

184

183

185

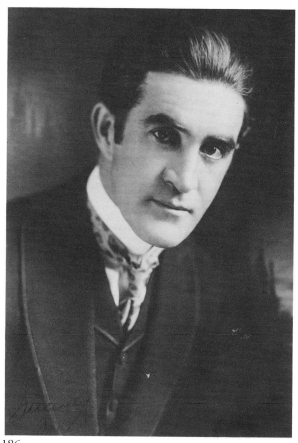

186

187

186. Francis Ford (1882–1953). Older brother of director John, Francis Ford also directed films in the silent era and was a memorable drunk both on screen and off. Films include *The Invaders* (1912), *The Campbells Are Coming* (1915), *The Craving* (1918), *The Man From Nowhere* (1920), *Thundering Hoofs* (1922), *Scar Hanan* (1925), and *Uncle Tom's Cabin* (1927).

187. Harrison Ford (1884–1957). On screen from the late 'teens and a frequent leading man to Marion Davies, Harrison Ford is no relation to the actor who currently bears that name. Films include *The Lottery Man* (1919), *Miss Hobbs* (1920), *Shadows* (1922), *Little Old New York* (1923), *Vanity Fair* (1923), *Janice Meredith* (1924), *That Royle Girl* (1925), and *Up in Mabel's Room* (1926).

188

189

188. Victoria Forde (1896–1964). Victoria Forde was closely associated with Tom Mix, becoming his leading lady at Selig in 1915 and his wife from 1918 to 1931. Films include *The $5,000 Elopement* (1916), *Local Color* (1916), *Some Duel* (1916), *The Cowboy God Forgot* (1916), and *Western Blood* (1918). **189. Tom Forman** (1891–1951). A reliable leading man — one critic aptly described him as "a comfortable man" — initially with Famous Players-Lasky; he was also a director. Films include *Young Romance* (1915), *Sweet Kitty Bellairs* (1916), *The American Consul* (1917), *The Sea Wolf* (1920), *Cappy Ricks* (1921), *Shadows* (1922), *The Virginian* (1923), and *Kosher Kitty Kelly* (1926).

190

191

190. Ann Forrest (1897–????). Ann Forrest was a Danish-born actress who began her screen career in 1918 after gaining an enthusiasm for motion pictures from watching "Broncho Billy" Anderson's Westerns in her native land. Films include *The Rainbow Trail* (1918), *The Prince Chap* (1920), *The Faith Healer* (1921), *The Man Who Played God* (1922), *If Winter Comes* (1923), and *Ridin' Pretty* (1925).

191. Earle Foxe (1891–1973). Foxe began his career at Kalem and by 1917 boasted of holding the record for having been leading man to the greatest number of stars: from Pearl White to Olga Petrova. He later ran the Black Foxe Military Academy in Hollywood. Films include *The Trail of the Lonesome Pine* (1916), *Panthea* (1917), *Peck's Bad Girl* (1918), *The Prodigal Judge* (1922), *Vanity Fair* (1923), *The Last Man on Earth* (1924), *A Trip to Chinatown* (1926), and *Four Sons* (1928).

192

193

192. Alec B. Francis (1867–1934). A dignified, older, English-born supporting actor, Alec B. Francis was on screen from the early 'teens until his death. Films include *The Wishing Ring* (1914), *Alias Jimmy Valentine* (1915), *The Cinderella Man* (1917), *The World and Its Woman* (1919), *The Butterfly Man* (1920), *Beyond the Rocks* 1922), *Beau Brummell* (1924), and *Camille* (1927).

193. Pauline Frederick (1881–1938). A mature actress with kindly, yet firm features, Pauline Frederick was the screen's second and best-known *Madam X* (1920) and gives what is undoubtedly her finest performance in *Smouldering Fires* (1924). Films include *The Eternal City* (1915; her first film), *Bella Donna* (1915), *Resurrection* (1918), *Three Women* (1924), *Mumsie* (1927), and *Thank You, Mr. Moto* (1937; her last film).

194

194. Dale Fuller (–). Dale Fuller was an elegant and icy cold leading lady of the twenties usually found in the films of Erich von Stroheim. Films include *Foolish Wives* (1922), *Merry-Go-Round*, (1923), *The Marriage Circle (1924)*, *Greed* (1925), *The Merry Widow* (1925), *The Canadian* (1926), *The King of Kings* (1927), and *The Wedding March*, (1928).   **195. Mary Fuller** (1893–????). Mary Fuller was the star of what is considered the forerunner to all serials, *What Happened to Mary?* (1912). She was a leading member of the Edison Company until 1914 when she joined Universal; her career did not last beyond the late 'teens. Films include *Mary Stuart* (1913), *Who Will Mary Marry?* (1913), *The Active Life of Dolly of the Dailies* (1914), *Under Southern Skies* (1914), *A Hunter of Men* (1916), and *The Long Trail* (1917).

195

196

196. Greta Garbo (1905–). A beautiful, cold, and strangely unemotional actress who made her American screen debut with *The Torrent* (1926). From then until her retirement with *Two-Faced Woman* (1941), she built a reputation that has made her legendary. Films include *The Temptress* (1926), *Love* (1927), *A Woman of Affairs* (1928), *Wild Orchids* (1929), and *The Kiss* (1929).

197

198

197. Helen Gardner (????–1968). Helen Gardner entered films with Vitagraph in 1911, and a year later, she formed her own company with husband/director Charles Gaskill. Her later career also included directing at Vitagraph and elsewhere. Films include *Vanity Fair* (1911), *Cleopatra* (1912), *A Sister to Carmen* (1913), *The Strange Story of Sylvia Grey* (1914), *The Breath of Araby* (1915), *The Sleep of Cyma Roget* (1920), *Devil's Angel* (1922), and *Sandra* (1924).   **198. Pauline Garon** (1900–1965). In films from the late 'teens, Pauline Garon was Cecil B. DeMille's first blonde heroine — in *Adam's Rib* (1923) — and was hailed as "The Perfect Flapper." Films include *Sonny* (1922), *Wine of Youth* (1924), *Fighting Youth* (1925), *The Love of Sunya* (1927), and *Her Husband's Secretary* (1937; her last film).

199

200

199. Gene Gauntier (1891–1966). A pioneering actress who joined the Kalem Company when it was founded in 1907, not only as its leading lady, but also as its principal screenwriter. Gene Gauntier formed her own company after leaving Kalem in 1912 and retired from films in the mid-'teens. Films include *The Little Spreewald Maiden* (1910), *Rory O'More* (1911), *The Colleen Bawn* (1911), *From the Manger to the Cross* (1912), and *Come Back to Erin* (1914).

200. Howard Gaye (????–1955). A British-born actor who commenced his career at Kalem in 1912 working with Carlyle Blackwell; he played Christ in *Intolerance* (1916). Howard Gaye made little impact either in the U. S. or in the U. K., where he returned in the twenties. Films include *The Birth of a Nation* (1915), *Daphne and the Pirate* (1916), *The Spy* (1917), *The Spirit of '76* (1918), *To Please One Woman* (1920), *Sacred and Profane Love* (1921), *Scaramouche* (1922), and *Dante's Inferno* (1924; his last U. S. film).

201

201. **Janet Gaynor** (1906–1984). In films from 1924, Janet Gaynor was, without question, the cutest star of late silents and early talkies. She was usually partnered with Charles Farrell, and was at her best in *7th Heaven* (1927) and *Sunrise — A Song of Two Humans* (1927). Films include *The Johnstown Flood* (1926), *Street Angel* (1928), *Four Devils* (1928), *Sunnyside Up* (1929), *A Star is Born* (1937), and *Bernadine* (1957; her last film). She appears in these photographs as she looked at the beginning and at the end of her starring screen career.

202

203

202. Maude George (1888–1963). A stylish leading lady with distinctive features, Maude George entered films at Universal in 1915 and later gained renown as a leading lady in the films of Erich von Stroheim. Films include *The Frame-Up* (1915), *Heart Strings* (1917), *Blue Blazes Rawden* (1918), *The Devil's Passkey* (1920), *Roads of Destiny* (1921), *Foolish Wives* (1922), *Monte Cristo* (1922), *Merry-Go-Round* (1923), *The Garden of Eden* (1928), and *The Wedding March* (1928).

203. Hoot Gibson (1892–1962). A popular Universal cowboy star of the late 'teens and twenties, Hoot Gibson remained active through the fifties. Films include *Action* (1921), *Headin' West* (1922), *Shootin' for Love* (1923), *Broadway or Bust* (1924), *Chip of the Flying U* (1926), and *Galloping Fury* (1927).

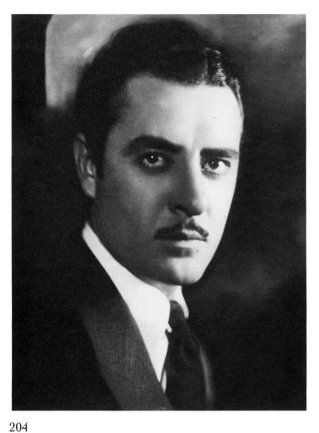

204

205

204. John Gilbert (1897–1936). From an extra in Thomas Ince productions of the mid-'teens, John Gilbert graduated to stardom as a sophisticated leading man of the twenties. His career took a disastrous turn when contemporary audiences found his voice inadequate for his screen image. He was married to actress Leatrice Joy from 1921–1924. Films include *Monte Cristo* (1922), *Cameo Kirby* (1923), *The Big Parade* (1925), *The Merry Widow* (1925), *La Bohème (1926)*, *Flesh and the Devil* (1926), *Love* (1927), *A Woman of Affairs* (1928), and *Queen Christina* (1933).

205. Claude Gillingwater (1870–1939). Claude Gillingwater was a slim and starch character actor, very busy on screen from the late 'teens until his death. Films include *Wild Primrose* (1918), *Little Lord Fauntleroy* (1921), *Alice Adams* (1923), *Daddies* (1924), *Seven Sinners* (1925), and *Barbed Wire* (1927).

206

207

206. Dorothy Gish (1898–1968). Lillian Gish's younger sister had an acting range for which she is seldom given credit. She could be amusing as in *Hearts of the World* (1918), she could be tender as in *Orphans of the Storm* (1922), and she could be a charming character player as in *Our Hearts Were Young and Gay* (1944). On stage from 1902, Dorothy Gish was discovered by D. W. Griffith and made her screen debut with the American Biograph Company in 1912; she was seen on screen through *The Cardinal* in 1964. Films include *An Unseen Enemy* (1912), *Old Heidelberg* (1915), *Boots* (1919), *Remodeling Her Husband* (1920), *Flying Pat* (1920), *The Bright Shawl* (1923), *Romola* (1924), *Nell Gwyn* (1926), and *Madame Pompadour* (1927).

207. Lillian Gish (1896–). To criticize Lillian Gish, as one writer noted, would be tantamount to denying God, one's mother, and one's country in a single breath. But who would want to criticize Lillian Gish, a legendary star who has been on screen since 1912 and is the greatest of all D. W. Griffith's leading ladies. In a raucous world, there is comfort in the dignity of Lillian Gish's appearances from the golden age of the silent cinema through the present era. Films include *The Mothering Heart* (1913), *The Birth of a Nation* (1915), *Hearts of the World* (1918), *True Heart Susie* (1919), *Broken Blossoms* (1919), *Way Down East* (1920), *Orphans of the Storm* (1921), *The White Sister* (1923), *La Bohème* (1926), and *The Wind* (1928). Autobiography: *The Movies, Mr. Griffith and Me* (Englewood Cliffs, NJ: Prentice-Hall, 1969). She appears in the first photograph (above), taken by Hendrick Sartov in 1918; and in the second photograph (right), taken by Abbé in 1923.

208

208. Louise Glaum (????–1970). A leading lady with Pathé and Nestor (1911–1912), Louise Glaum first came to notice working with Thomas Ince. She is memorable as the vamp who leads William S. Hart astray in *Hell's Hinges* (1916) and at her outrageous best in *Sex* (1920). Films include *The Aryan* (1916), *Sahara* (1919), *The Lone Wolf's Daughter* (1920), and *Greater Than Love* (1921).   **209. Julia Swayne Gordon** (1878–1933). Julia Swayne Gordon began her career at Edison, but she gained fame at Vitagraph from 1909–1918. Later, she was memorable as Richard Arlen's mother in *Wings* (1927). Films include *The Battle Hymn of the Republic* (1911), *A Million Dollar Bid* (1914), *The Juggernaut* (1915), *The Battle Cry of Peace* (1915), *My Old Kentucky Home* (1922), *Scaramouche* (1923), *Bride of the Storm* (1926), and *It* (1927).

209

210. Kitty Gordon (1878–1974). A major stage star for whom Victor Herbert wrote his operetta, *The Enchantress*, in 1911, Kitty Gordon was active in the 'teens and ended her career on television in 1952. She was noted for the beauty of her back. Films include *The Crucial Test* (1916), *Forget-Me-Not* (1917), *The Wasp* (1918), and *The Scar* (1919).

210

211

211. Jetta Goudal (1891–1985). A vision of aristocratic loveliness on screen from 1922 through 1932, Jetta Goudal gave the same meticulous care to her film characterizations as she had done earlier in her stage career. Extremely temperamental both on and off screen, recent research indicates that she was not of French ancestry, but a Dutch Jew. Films include *Timothy's Quest* (1922; her first film), *The Bright Shawl* (1923), *Salome of the Tenements* (1925), *The Road to Yesterday* (1925), *Three Faces East* (1926), *White Gold* (1927), *Lady of the Pavements* (1929), and *Business and Pleasure* (1932; her last film).

212

213

212. Ethel Grandin (1894–1988). The star of the first two-reel film produced in Los Angeles, *War on the Plains* (1912), and the star of the cinema's first sex exploitation drama, *Traffic in Souls* (1913), Ethel Grandin was a charming and petite actress, quite rightly dubbed "The Imp of the IMP Company." Films include *Blazing Trail* (1912), *Jane Eyre* (1914), *The Crimson Stain Mystery* (1916 serial), and *A Tailor-Made Man* (1922; her last film).   **213. Valentine Grant** (1881–1949). When director Sidney Olcott and leading lady Gene Gauntier parted company in 1914, the former tried to substitute his wife-to-be, Valentine Grant, as the star of his films. This idea did not work, despite Grant's assertion that "I would make every one of my character portraits absolutely real and true." Films include *Bold Emmett, Ireland's Martyr* (1915), *The Melting Pot* (1915), *The Innocent Lie* (1916), and *The Belgian* (1918).

215

214

214. Ralph Graves (1900–1977). A husky leading man with a face that seemed more suited to comedy than drama, Ralph Graves was in silent films from the late 'teens and on screen through the early talkies. Films include *Men Who Have Made Love to Me* (1918), *Sporting Life* (1919), *The White Heather* (1919), *Scarlet Days* (1919), *The Greatest Question* (1919), *Dream Street* (1921), *The Extra Girl* (1923), *That Certain Thing* (1928), and *Ladies of Leisure* (1930).   **215. Cesare Gravina** (1858–????). Cesare Gravina was an Italian-born character actor in U. S. films of the 'teens and twenties. His ugly, almost deformed features were particularly attractive to Erich von Stroheim. Films include *Madame Butterfly* (1915), *Poor Little Peppina* (1916), *Miss Nobody* (1917), *Madame X* (1920), *Foolish Wives* (1922), *The Hunchback of Notre Dame* (1923), *The Phantom of the Opera* (1925), *The Man Who Laughs* (1927), and *The Wedding March* (1928).

216

217

216. Corinne Griffith (1894–1979). Corinne Griffith's claim to fame may not simply be that she was a major Hollywood star of the twenties, but rather that in later years, she claimed not to be Corinne Griffith at all, but her stand-in, who took over when the real Corinne Griffith died in the mid-thirties. She worked for Vitagraph from 1916 through 1922 and had her own production company releasing through First National from 1924 through 1930. Films include *The Yellow Girl* (1916), *Thin Ice* (1919), *The Common Law* (1923), *Six Days* (1923), *Lilies of the Field*, (1924), *Black Oxen* (1924), *Déclassée* (1925), *The Garden of Eden* (1928), *Lily Christine* (1932), and *Stars in the Backyard* (1957; her last film).

217. Raymond Griffith (1890–1957). A restrained, silent comedian with a well-deserved but small cult following, Raymond Griffith turned from acting to producing with the coming of sound. Films include *Open All Night* (1924), *Paths to Paradise* (1925), *Hands Up!* (1926), and *All Quiet on the Western Front* (1930; his last film as an actor).

218

218. William Haines (1900–1973). A top M-G-M
star of light comedy in the late twenties, William
Haines' career ended supposedly when his homosexual-
ity became too much of an embarrassment for the
studio. He later switched careers to became a highly
regarded interior decorator. Films include *Brothers
Under the Skin* (1922; his first film), *Wine of Youth*
(1924), *Brown of Harvard* (1926), *Tell It to the Marines*
(1926), *West Point* (1927), *Show People* (1928), and *Alias
Jimmy Valentine* (1929).   **219. Alan Hale** (1892–1950).
A likeable leading man whose career began in 1911,
Alan Hale was a perfect Little John to Fairbanks' *Robin
Hood* (1922). Films include *The Power of the Press*
(1914), *Dora Thorne* (1915), *Pudd'nhead Wilson* (1916),
Life's Whirlpool (1917), *The Barbarian* (1920), *The Four
Horsemen of the Apocalypse* (1921), *The Covered Wagon*
(1923), *Dick Turpin* (1925), and *Rubber Tires* (1927).

219

220

220. Creighton Hale (1882–1965). A dashing serial hero opposite Pearl White, Creighton Hale became typecast as a foolish leading man in D. W. Griffith features. He ended his career as a character player.

Films include *The Exploits of Elaine* (1915), *Charity* (1916), *Way Down East* (1920), *Trilby* (1923), *The Marriage Circle* (1924), *Beverly of Graustark* (1926), and *The Cat and the Canary* (1927).

221

222

221. Ella Hall (1896–1981). Ella Hall was a pretty, Universal star of the 'teens noted for her large blue eyes and capacity for portraying child roles, most notably in Lois Weber's *Jewel* (1915). Films include *The Spy* (1914), *The Bugler of Algiers* (1916), *The Charmer* (1917), *The Heart of Rachael* (1918), *Under the Top* (1919), *The Third Alarm* (1922), and *The Flying Dutchman* (1923).

222. James Hall (1900–1940). A somewhat tepid leading man, best remembered for losing his girlfriend, Jean Harlow, to Ben Lyon in *Hell's Angels* (1930). Films include *The Campus Flirt* (1926), *Hotel Imperial* (1927), *Rolled Stockings* (1927), and *Four Sons* (1928).

223

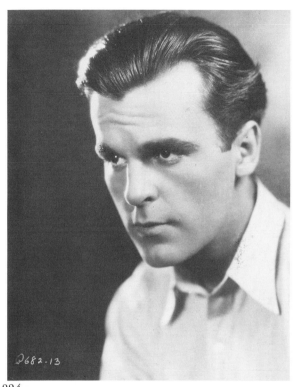

224

223. Lloyd Hamilton (1891–1935). One-half of the Kalem "Ham and Bud" comedies (1914–1917) with Albert Duncan, Lloyd Hamilton developed a career as a single in Fox Sunshine Comedies and in his own productions, released through Educational, in the twenties. Films include *Ham in the Harem* (1915), *Ham at the Garbage Gentleman's Ball* (1915), *A Twilight Baby* (1918), *The Mischief Man* (1920), *His Darker Self* (1924), and *The Rainmaker* (1926).

224. Neil Hamilton (1899–1984). A male model (The Arrow Collar Man), Neil Hamilton was discovered by D. W. Griffith in 1923 and was under contract to Paramount from 1925 through 1930. A competent, yet undemonstrative leading man, he was at his best in *Isn't Life Wonderful* (1924), and *Beau Geste* (1926). Films include *The White Rose* (1923), *America* (1924), *Diplomacy* (1926), *The Great Gatsby* (1926), *Ten Modern Commandments* (1927), *Mother Machree* (1928), and *The Patriot* (1928).

225

226

225. **Elaine Hammerstein** (1898–1948). The daughter of theatrical impressario Arthur Hammerstein, she supposedly entered films to escape the stage. Films include *The Moonstone* (1915), *The Argyle Case* (1917), *Her Man* (1918), *The Country Cousin* (1919), *The Daughter Pays* (1920), *Reckless Youth* (1922), *Souls for Sale* (1923), *Paint and Powder* (1925), and *Ladies of Leisure* (1926). 226. **Hope Hampton** (1897–1982). A legendary society lady dubbed "The Duchess of Park Avenue," Hope Hampton retired from silent films in favor of a dubious career in opera; more a celebrity than an actress to be taken seriously. Films include *A Modern Salome* (1920), *Love's Penalty*, (1921), *The Light in the Dark* (1922), *The Gold Diggers* (1923), *The Truth About Women* (1924), *Fifty-Fifty* (1925), and *The Unfair Sex* (1926).   227. **Juanita Hansen** (1895–1961). Juanita Hansen was a little remembered, but important serial star — *The Secret of the Submarine* (1916), *The Phantom Foe* (1920), *The Yellow Arm* (1921), etc. — whose career suffered as a result of drug addiction and ended when her face was severely scarred by scalding water. Films include *The Patchwork Girl of Oz* (1914), *The Mediator* (1916), *Glory* (1917), *The Mating of Marcella* (1918), *The Poppy Girl's Husband* (1919), and *The Jungle Princess* (1920). **Oliver Hardy**, see entry No. 286.

227

228

228. Sam Hardy (1883–1935). Sam Hardy was the screen's low-class "man of the world" who almost became a star in silents, but he was demoted to character roles in talkies. Films include *Judy Forgot* (1915), *A Woman's Experience* (1919), *Get-Rich-Quick-Wallingford* (1921), *Little Old New York* (1923), *When Love Grows Cold* (1925), *The Savage* (1926), and *Orchids and Ermine* (1927).

229

230

229. Kenneth Harlan (1895–1967). A dependable leading man, Kenneth Harlan's film career lasted from the mid-'teens through the early forties and included marriage to his leading lady, Marie Prevost (one of his seven wives). Films include *Betsy's Buglar* (1917), *The Flame of the Yukon* (1917), *The Hoodlum* (1919), *The Penalty* (1920), *Polly of the Follies* (1922), *The Toll of the Sea* (1922), *Little Church Around the Corner* (1923), *The Virginian* (1923), *Bobbed Hair* (1925), and *Cheating Cheaters* (1927).

230. Otis Harlan (1865–1940). A plump and jolly character actor on screen through the thirties, Otis Harlan was the voice of Happy in *Snow White and the Seven Dwarfs* (1937). Films include *A Black Sheep* (1915), *The Girl in the Taxi* (1921), *The World's a Stage* (1922), *Main Street* (1923), *Captain Blood* (1924), *Dollar Down* (1925), *The Prince of Pilsen* (1926), and *The Student Prince in Old Heidelberg* (1927).

231

232

231. Mildred Harris (1901–1944). The first wife of Charles Chaplin (1918–1920), Mildred Harris entered films in the late 'teens and came to stardom under the guidance of Lois Weber. She worked in vaudeville and nightclubs after her silent career ended and was on screen in "bit" parts until her death. Films include *The Old Folks at Home* (1916), *The Price of a Good Time* (1917), *The Doctor and the Woman* (1918), *Polly of the Storm Country* (1920), *The Fog* (1923), and *The Cruise of the Jasper B* (1926).   **232. Robert Harron** (1893–1920). The maturation of Robert Harron's characters in *Intolerance* (1916) and *True Heart Susie* (1919) demonstrate what a magnificent dramatic actor he was; youth was no drawback in a career that began in 1907 and ended with a tragic, accidental shooting death. Films include *A Misunderstood Boy* (1912), *The Birth of a Nation* (1915), *Hearts of the World* (1918), *A Romance of Happy Valley* (1918), and *Coincidence* (1921; his last film).

233

233. **William S. Hart** (1865–1946). A sombre, middle-aged actor, William S. Hart brought a lifetime of theatrical experience to the Western films in which he starred from 1914–1925. His films were not glamorous like those of Tom Mix, but they had an air of honesty and respect for the West. Films include *The Bargain* (1914), *Hell's Hinges* (1916), *The Captive God* (1916), *Blue Blazes Rawden* (1918), *The Toll Gate* (1920), *The Whistle* (1921), and *Tumbleweeds* (1925; his last film). Autobiography: *My Life East and West* (Boston: Houghton Mifflin, 1929). William S. Hart (second from right) appears in this photograph with artist James Montgomery Flagg, boxer Jack Dempsey, and director Erle C. Kenton in 1923.   **234. Raymond Hatton** (1887–1971). A long-time DeMille supporting player of the 'teens, Raymond Hatton was teamed in a series of comedies opposite Wallace Beery during the late twenties. Films include *The Warrens of Virginia* (1915), *Joan the Woman* (1916), *Nan of Music Mountain* (1917), *Arizona* (1918), *Male and Female* (1919), *Officer 666* (1920), *Peck's Bad Boy* (1921), *The Hunchback of Notre Dame* (1923), *Behind the Front* (1926), and *Fashions for Women* (1927).

234

235

235. Phyllis Haver (1899–1960). An attractive and perky blonde, Phyllis Haver began her career as a Mack Sennett Bathing Beauty in 1917 and was active through 1929. Films include *A Small Town Idol* (1921), *The Christian* (1923), *Lilies of the Field* (1924), *Up in Mabel's Room* (1926), *Fig Leaves* (1926), *What Price Glory* (1926), *The Way of All Flesh* (1927), and *The Battle of the Sexes* (1928). **236. Wanda Hawley** (1895–1963). A petite actress who became one of Cecil B. DeMille's mistresses; with the demise of her film career in 1931, she became a San Francisco call girl. Films include *The Heart of a Lion* (1917), *Mr. Fix-It* (1918), *Peg o' My Heart* (1919), *Miss Hobbs* (1920), *The Young Rajah* (1922), and *Smouldering Fires* (1925).

236

237

238

237. Sessue Hayakawa (1889–1973). A Japanese actor of extraordinary power, whether in *The Cheat* (1915) or *The Bridge On the River Kwai* (1957). Films include *The Wrath of the Gods* (1914; his first film), *The Honor of His House* (1918), *The Tong Man* (1919), and *The Vermilion Pencil* (1922). Autobiography: *Zen Showed Me the Way* (Indianapolis: Bobbs-Merrill, 1960).

238. Gale Henry (1893–1972). An eccentric comedienne who began her career in shorts at Universal in 1914 and formed her own production company in 1919. Films include *Lady Baffles and Detective Duck* (1915), *A Wild Woman* (1919), *The Hunch* (1921), *Quincy Adams Sawyer* (1922), *Merton of the Movies* (1924), *Déclassée* (1925), and *Stranded* (1927).

239

240

239. Jean Hersholt (1886–1956). One of the screen's best known character actors, Jean Hersholt will always be associated with the role of Dr. Christian in films and on radio (1936–1948). He began his American career with Thomas Ince in 1915, and his most important silent role was as Schouler in *Greed* (1925). Films include *The Terror* (1917), *'49–'17* (1917), *Princess Virtue* (1917), *Madame Spy* (1918), *The Four Horsemen of the Apocalypse* (1921), *Tess of the Storm Country* (1922), *Don Q, Son of Zorro* (1925), *Stella Dallas* (1925), *The Student Prince in Old Heidelberg* (1927), *The Battle of the Sexes* (1928), and more than sixty sound features.   **240. Walter Hiers** (1893–1933). Always busy, Walter Hiers was a heavy-weight supporting comedian who seldom raises a laugh with modern audiences. Films include *Just Out of College* (1915), *Seventeen* (1916), *Brown of Harvard* (1918), *It Pays to Advertise* (1919), *So Long Letty* (1920), *Her Gilded Cage* (1922), *Christine of the Hungry Heart* (1924), and *A Racing Romeo* (1927).

241

242

241. Johnny Hines (1898–1970). A light comedian of the twenties whose films have not stood the test of time, Johnny Hines was featured in a series of "Torchy" comedies in the late 'teens and early twenties. He was active as an actor through the thirties. Films include *Burn 'Em Up Barnes* (1921), *Little Johnny Jones* (1923), *The Live Wire* (1925), and *The Brown Derby* (1926).

242. Helen Holmes (1892–1950). Helen Holmes entered films with Keystone circa 1912 and then moved to the Kalem Company, where she married director J. P. McGowan and became the star of the serial *The Hazards of Helen* (1914–1915). Films include *Lass of the Lumberlands* (1916 serial), *The Lost Express* (1917 serial), *The Railroad Raiders* (1917 serial), *The Fatal Fortune* (1919 serial), *The Lone Hand* (1922), *Fighting Fury* (1924), and *Crossed Signals* (1926).

243

244

243. Stuart Holmes (1884–1971). Described by *Photoplay* magazine as early as 1916 as "an admirable villain," Stuart Holmes added a touch of dash to his villainous roles whether as Black Michael in *The Prisoner of Zenda* (1922) or as Alec D'Uberville in *Tess of the D'Urbervilles* (1924). He was on screen from the mid-'teens through the sixties. Films include *The Wild Girl* (1916), *The New Moon* (1919), *The Way of a Woman* (1919), *The Four Horsemen of the Apocalypse* (1921), *Under Two Flags* (1922), *Three Weeks* (1924), and *The Salvation Hunters* (1925). **244. Jack Holt** (1888–1951). Jack Holt was a competent actor who played any type of hero in silent films, but he became best known for his action roles in talkies. He was on screen through the fifties. Films include *Jewel* (1915), *The Dumb Girl of Portici* (1916), *The Little American* (1917), *The Squaw Man* (1918), *Victory* (1919), *The Mask* (1921), *Making a Man* (1922), *Hollywood* (1923), *North of '36* (1924), *The Thundering Herd* (1925), and *The Warning* (1927).

245

245. Hedda Hopper (1890–1966). Noted for her portrayal of vamps in the 'teens, Hedda Hopper took her name from husband DeWolf Hopper (married 1913–1921). As her film career declined in the thirties, she became a prominent gossip columnist until her death. Films include *Seven Keys to Baldpate* (1917), *The Third Degree* (1919), *Conceit* (1921), *Sherlock Holmes* (1922), *Reno* (1923), *The Snob* (1924), *Zander the Great* (1925), *Don Juan* (1926), and *Orchids and Ermine* (1927). Autobiography: *From Under My Hat* (Garden City, NY: Doubleday, 1952). She appears in this photograph in a parody of the "Mona Lisa."

246. Camilla Horn (1907–). Camilla Horn was an attractive German-born star who made her debut in F. W. Murnau's *Faust* (1926) — she came to the U. S. to star in three features — *Tempest* (1928), *Eternal Love* (1929), and *The Royal Box* (1929) — of which only the first two were silent.

247. Edward Everett Horton (1886–1970). A funny, slightly effeminate supporting actor in talkies until his death, Edward Everett Horton was an excellent light comedian in silent features from 1922 onward, most notably in *Beggar on Horseback* (1925). Films include *Ruggles of Red Gap* (1923), *Flapper Wives* (1924), *Marry Me* (1925), *La Bohème* (1926), and *Taxi! Taxi!* (1927). **248. Alice Howell** (1889–1961). Stan Laurel ranked this underrated actress as one of the cinema's ten greatest comediennes. From the mid-'teens through the mid-twenties, Alice Howell's grotesque characterizations, body movements, and facial expressions highlighted dozens of minor two-reel comedies. **249. Al Hoxie** (1902–1892). A mediocre cowboy star, Al Hoxie made his debut in the 1920 serial *Thunderbolt Jack*. He came to stardom in features for Morris Schlank's Anchor Productions, followed by Bud Barsky's Wild West Pictures and Krelbar Productions, companies whose names suggest the lack of quality. Films include *The Ace of Clubs* (1926), *Smoking Guns* (1927), and *Outlawed* (1928).

248

247

249

250

250. Louise Huff (1896–1973). A Paramount star of the late 'teens who first came to prominence with the Lubin Company, Louise Huff was known as "The Kate Greenaway Girl of the Screen." Films include *Caprice* (1913), *Seventeen* (1916), *Great Expectations* (1917), *Tom Sawyer* (1917), *Jack and Jill* (1917), *What Women Want* (1920), and *Disraeli* (1921).

251

252

251. Lloyd Hughes (1897–1958). Lloyd Hughes entered films in January, 1917, and became the screen's quintessential American youth: clean-cut, wholesome, and rather dull. Films include *Impossible Susan* (1918), *The Heart of Humanity* (1919), *Dangerous Hours* (1920), *Hail the Woman* (1921), *Tess of the Storm Country* (1922), *The Sea Hawk* (1924), *The Lost World* (1925), *Ella Cinders* (1926), and *Moby Dick* (1930).

252. Gladys Hulette (1896–). A pioneering screen actress who starred in two very different, major films twelve years apart: *Princess Nicotine* (1909) and *Tol'able David* (1921). Films include *The Iron Horse* (1924), *Lena Rivers* (1925), and *A Bowery Cinderella* (1927).

253

254

253. William J. Humphrey (1875–1942). An actor and director at Vitagraph from 1909 through 1917, William J. Humphrey specialized in the portrayal of Napoleon. After a brief directing career in the late 'teens, he returned to acting in the twenties. Films include *Incidents in the Life of Napoleon and Josephine* (1909), *A Tale of Two Cities* (1911), *Mr. Barnes of New York* (1914), *From Out of the Past* (1916), *Scaramouche* (1923), *Abraham Lincoln* (1924), and *Midnight Limited* (1926).

254. Madeline Hurlock (1899–1989). An attractive foil at Mack Sennett — often in vamp roles — from 1923 onwards to Ben Turpin, Andy Clyde, Harry Langdon, and (later) Laurel and Hardy. Madeline Hurlock was married to two noted literary figures: first to Marc Connelly and later to Robert Sherwood. Films include *The Daredevil* (1923), *The Prodigal Bridegroom* (1926), and *Duck Soup* (1927).

255

256

257

255. Paul Hurst (1888–1953). A leading "heavy" in both silent and sound films, Paul Hurst was memorable as the "Yankee deserter" in *Gone with the Wind* (1939). He made his screen debut at Kalem in 1912. Films include *Shannon of the Sixth* (1914), *The Pitfall* (1916), *Rimrock Jones* (1918), *The Heart of the Texan* (1922), *Roaring Road* (1926), and *The Overland Stage* (1927). **256. Peggy Hyland** (–). A pretty, English-born Vitagraph star of the late 'teens who disappeared from the screen in 1923. Films include *The Enemy* (1919), *Womanhood, The Glory of a Nation* (1917), *Miss Adventure* (1919), *Black Shadows* (1920), *The Price of Silence* (1921), and *Shifting Sands* (1923). **257. Emil Jannings** (1894–1950). In a particular type of silent dramatic role, Emil Jannings was unsurpassed, as in *The Last Laugh* (1924), *Variety* (1925), and *The Last Command* (1928). On screen in his native Germany (although he was actually born in Switzerland) from the mid-'teens, his last film of impact to reach the U. S. was *The Blue Angel* (1930). Films include *The Way of All Flesh* (1927; his first U. S. film), *The Patriot* (1928), and *Betrayal* (1929).

258

258. Jean (????–1916). The first dog star, Jean entered films at Vitagraph circa 1909 with her owner, Larry Trimble. The *Vitagraph Bulletin* (October 15, 1910) commented: "Jean is an inspiration; no-one could help making a fine story about her, and no actor could act badly in her support." Films include *Jean and the Calico Doll* (1910), *Jean Goes Fishing* (1910), *Jean Rescues* (1911), and *Jean Intervenes* (1912).

259

260

260. Julanne Johnston (1906–). Formerly a solo dancer with Ruth St. Denis, Julanne Johnston always exhibited the graceful movements of her profession on screen. Films include *The Brass Bottle* (1923), *The Thief of Bagdad* (1924), *Big Pal* (1925), *Aloma of the South Seas* (1926), and *Her Wild Oat* (1927).

259. Arthur Johnson (1877–1916). D. W. Griffith, with whom Arthur Johnson made his debut in *The Adventures of Dollie* (1908), called this actor "matchless in everything — modern, romantic, comedy. He would have been a great film leader had he lived." He was at Lubin from 1911–1916 and usually co-starred with Lottie Briscoe. Films include *Edgar Allan Poe* (1908), *A Corner in Wheat* (1909), *In Old California* (1911), *The Beloved Adventurer* (1914), and *Country Blood* (1915).

261

262

261. Buck Jones (1889–1942). Perhaps the only cowboy star to display any sensitivity on screen, Buck Jones was initially hired by Fox in 1920 as a possible replacement for Tom Mix. He gives beautiful performances in *Just Pals* (1920) and *Lazybones* (1925). Films include *Straight From the Shoulder* (1921), *Pardon My Nerve!* (1922), *The Desert Outlaw* (1924), *Desert Valley* (1926), and *Whispering Sage* (1927).

262. Leatrice Joy (1899–1985). A pleasant ingénue, Leatrice Joy was a model who began her screen career as an extra in 1917. She was married to actor John Gilbert from 1921 to 1924 and was a Cecil B. DeMille contract star from 1922 to 1928. Films include *Bunty Pulls the Strings* (1921), *Manslaughter* (1922), *Java Head* (1923), *The Ten Commandments* (1923), *Eve's Leaves* (1926), and *The Angel of Broadway* (1927).

264

263

263. Alice Joyce (1890–1955). With a mature beauty, Alice Joyce was a talented, pioneering actress who began her screen career with Kalem in 1911. At one time, she was billed as "The Madonna of the Screen." Early in her career, she was married to actor Tom Moore; after her retirement from films, she married director Clarence Brown. Films include *The Beast* (1914), *Whom the Gods Destroy* (1916), *Womanhood, The Glory of a Nation* (1917), *Within the Law* (1917), *The Lion and the Mouse* (1919), *The Green Goddess* (1923), *Stella Dallas* (1925), *Dancing Mothers* (1926), *Beau Geste* (1926), *Sorrell and Son* (1927), *Song o' My Heart* (1930), and *He Knew Women* (1930; her last film). **264. Buster Keaton** (1895–1966). A vaudevillian who entered films in 1917, Buster Keaton has been rediscovered in recent years and acclaimed as the greatest of all the silent comedians. He was good and is still funny, but perhaps not as innovative as Harold Lloyd nor as understanding in the use of comedy as Chaplin. Films include *The Butcher's Boy* (1917), *Our Hospitality* (1923), *Sherlock, Jr.* (1924), *The Navigator* (1924), *Go West* (1925), *The General* (1927), and *The Cameraman* (1928). Autobiography: *My Wonderful World of Slapstick* (Garden City, NY: Doubleday, 1960).

265

266

267

265. Zena Keefe (1896–1977). An attractive, very young ingénue at Vitagraph from 1909 through 1916, Zena Keefe became a Selznick star of the late 'teens, retiring in 1924. Films include *The Light That Failed* (1912), *The Cross Roads* (1912), *The Mill of the Gods* (1912), *The Tigress* (1915), *Enlighten Thy Daughter* (1917), *Piccadilly Jim* (1920), *After Midnight* (1921), *When Love Is Young* (1922), and *The Broken Violin* (1923). **266. Frank Keenan** (1858–1929). Frank Keenan was a stage character actor who came to the screen at the insistence of producer Thomas H. Ince; he is memorable in *The Coward* (1915). Films include *Jim Grimsby's Boy* (1916), *The Bride of Hate* (1917), *The Bells* (1918), *Dollar for Dollar* (1920), *Lorna Doone* (1922), *East Lynne* (1925), and *The Gilded Butterfly* (1926). **267. Donald Keith** (1905–). He was an attractive twenties juvenile leading man, particularly well-cast as a college boy. Films include *Baree, Son of Kazan* (1925), *The Plastic Age* (1925), *Dancing Mothers* (1926), and *The Way of All Flesh* (1927).

268

DOROTHY KELLY
OF THE
VITAGRAPH PLAYERS

269

270

268. Annette Kellermann (1888–1975). Annette Kellermann was an Australian-born swimming star who graduated from vaudeville to films, first at Vitagraph in 1909 and then as a Fox star in *Neptune's Daughter* (1914), *A Daughter of the Gods* (1916), and *Queen of the Sea* (1918). She also starred in two non-Fox features, *What Women Love* (1920) and *Venus of the South Seas* (1924). Esther Williams portrayed her in a far-from-convincing film biography, *Million Dollar Mermaid* (1952).   **269. Dorothy Kelly** (1894–1966). A Vitagraph star from 1911 through 1916 when she retired from the screen. Films include *Vanity Fair* (1911), *The Troublesome Stepdaughters* (1912), *The Flirt* (1913), *Artie* (1916), and *The Maelstrom* (1916).

270. Madge Kennedy (1891–1987). A delightful stage comedienne (from 1910), Madge Kennedy's silent films generally failed to do her talent justice; she fared better on screen as a character actress from the fifties onwards. Her first 21 features, from 1917–1921, were produced by Samuel Goldwyn. Films include *Baby Mine* (1917; her first film), *The Service Star* (1918), *The Girl with a Jazz Heart* (1921), *Three Miles Out* (1924), *The Marrying Kind* (1952; start of career in talkies), and *Marathon Man* (1976; her last film).

272

271

271. Charles Kent (1852–1923). A distinguished
stage actor who joined Vitagraph as actor and director
in 1906, Charles Kent was a forceful presence on
screen until his death. Films include *Becket* (1910), *A
Tale of Two Cities* (1911), *The Battle Cry of Peace* (1915),
The Question (1917), *Wild Primrose* (1918), *Man and His
Woman* (1920), *The Charming Deceiver* (1921), and *The
Purple Highway* (1923). **272. Larry Kent** (1900–
1967). An American college-boy type whose film career
dated from the mid-twenties. Films include *Obey the Law*
(1926), *McFadden's Flats* (1927), and *Hangman's House*
(1928).

273

273. Doris Kenyon (1897–1979) and **Milton Sills** (1882–1930). Doris Kenyon and Milton Sills were married in 1927. The former played a silly ingénue in 'teens films; she matured to stardom in the twenties and continued in sound films as a well-spoken, aristocratic featured player. The screen fairly sizzles during her love scenes with Rudolph Valentino in *Monsieur Beaucaire* (1924). Films include *A Girl's Folly* (1917), *The Conquest of Canaan* (1921), *A Thief in Paradise* (1924), *Interference* (1929), *Alexander Hamilton* (1931), *Voltaire* (1933), and *The Man in the Iron Mask* (1939; her last film). Milton Sills was a somewhat older-than-average leading man who always seemed to have a strained expression on his face. Films include *The Pit* (1914; his first film), *Patria* (1916 serial), *The Honor System* (1917), *The Claw* (1918), *Eyes of Youth* (1919), *The Great Moment* (1920), *Adam's Rib* (1923), *The Spoilers* (1923), *The Sea Hawk* (1924), and *The Sea Wolf* (1930; his last film).

274

274. J. Warren Kerrigan (1879–1947). A somewhat effete leading man whose screen career began in 1909, Kerrigan came to prominence with the American Flying A Company (1910–1911) and then became a Universal contract star. Because of his suggestion that lesser mortals than he should be drafted during the First World War, he was dubbed "The Beautiful Slacker."

Never married, he lived with his mother, to whom he dedicated his autobiography. Films include *Samson* (1914), *The Measure of a Man* (1916), *A Man's Man* (1917), *The Joyous Liar* (1919), *The Covered Wagon* (1923), and *Captain Blood* (1924; his last film). Autobiography: *How I Became a Successful Moving Picture Star* (Los Angeles: self-published, 1914).

275

276

275. Norman Kerry (1889–1956). A colorful character by all accounts — at one time, he joined the French Foreign Legion — Norman Kerry was a somewhat melodramatic silent actor on screen through the forties. Films include *Manhattan Madness* (1916; his first film), *The Little Princess* (1917), *Amarilly of Clothes Line Alley* (1918), *Soldiers of Fortune* (1919), *The Hunchback of Notre Dame* (1923), *Cytherea* (1924), *The Phantom of the Opera* (1925), and *Annie Laurie* (1927). **276. Natalie Kingston** (–). She entered films in 1924 when she was spotted by the unlikely combination of Cecil B. DeMille and Mack Sennett, and was a leading lady to Harry Langdon in *All Night Long* (1924), *Feet of Mud* (1924), *Remember When* (1925), and *Soldier Man* (1926). Films include *Don Juan's Three Nights* (1926), *Kid Boots* (1926), *Framed* (1927), *A Girl in Every Port* (1928), and *Street Angel* (1928).

277

278

277. James Kirkwood (1875–1963). On screen from 1909 when he joined the American Biograph Company, James Kirkwood remained active until his death. He also did some directing. *Photoplay* magazine rightly described him as "one of those regular film 'troopers' who never fall down." Films include *Home, Sweet Home* (1914), *The Luck of the Irish* (1920), *Bob Hampton of Placer* (1921), *Human Wreckage* (1923), *That Royle Girl* (1925), *Butterflies in the Rain* (1926), and *Over the Hill* (1931).

278. Theodore Kosloff (1882–1956). One had only to look at Theodore Kosloff to agree with *Motion Picture* magazine's summation (May 1922): "the personification of temperament." Formerly with the Imperial Russian Ballet School, he was introduced to Cecil B. DeMille by Jeanie Macpherson and not only acted in the director's films, but also staged his orgy scenes. Films include *The Woman God Forgot* (1917; his first film), *Why Change Your Wife?* (1920), *The Affairs of Anatol* (1921), *Manslaughter* (1922), *Adam's Rib* (1923), *Feet of Clay* (1924), *Beggar on Horseback* (1925), and *The King of Kings* (1927).

279

280

279. Florence La Badie (1888–1917). She was the most important actress with the Thanhouser Company from 1911 until her death in an automobile accident in 1917. Films include *In the Chorus* (1911; her first film), *Dr. Jekyll and Mr. Hyde* (1912), *The Million Dollar Mystery* (1914), *Monsieur Lecoq* (1915), *The Fugitive* (1916), and *The Man Without a Country* (1917).

280. Alice Lake (1895–1967). Alice Lake entered films in the early 'teens, became a Mack Sennett leading lady, and graduated to stardom at Metro where she was often teamed with Bert Lytell. She was active through the early forties. Films include *The Moonstone* (1915; her first film), *The Lion's Den* (1919), *Should A Woman Tell?* (1920), *Body and Soul* (1920), *Shore Acres* (1920), *Uncharted Seas* (1921), and *The Angel of Broadway* (1927).

281

281. Arthur Lake (1905–1987). Arthur Lake was a juvenile leading man of the twenties often cast as a figure of fun. He gained fame in the thirties and forties as Dagwood Bumstead in the "Blondie" series for Columbia. Films include *Where Was I?* (1925), *Skinner's Dress Suit* (1926), *The Cradle Snatchers* (1927), *The Irresistible Lover* (1927), and *Harold Teen* (1928).

283

282

282. Barbara La Marr (1896–1926). A great silent screen beauty who died at the height of her fame, Barbara La Marr entered films in 1920 and was created a star by director Rex Ingram. Films include *Trifling Women* (1922), *The Eternal City* (1923), *The White Moth* (1924), and *The Girl From Montmartre* (1926; her last film).

283. Cullen Landis (1895–1975). Cullen Landis began in films as a truck driver in 1914. He worked as a prop man, assistant director, and stuntman before becoming an actor in the late 'teens. Somehow, he always acted as if he were a truck driver. Films include *Almost A Husband* (1919), *The Outcasts of Poker Flats* (1919), *It's a Great Life* (1920), *Bunty Pulls the Strings* (1921), *Soul of the Beast* (1923), *Pampered Youth* (1925), *My Old Dutch* (1926), and *Lights of New York* (1928).

284

284. Harry Langdon (1884–1944). A vaudevillian who entered films in 1924 and found that he could not play baby-faced innocents (with a dash of malice) forever. His films from 1930 onwards are depressing in their waste of an obviously misunderstood talent. Films include *Tramp, Tramp, Tramp* (1926), *The Strong Man* (1926), *Long Pants* (1927), and *The Chaser* (1928).

285. Laura La Plante (1904–). Short-cropped hair and an impish grin were the trademarks of this leading light comedienne at Universal from 1921–1930. She entered films with Christie Comedies in 1919 and was first noticed with her performance in *The Old Swimmin' Hole* (1921). Films include *The Thrill Chaser* (1923), *Butterfly* (1924), *Smouldering Fires* (1925), *Dangerous Innocence* (1925), *The Beautiful Cheat* (1926), *Skinner's Dress Suit* (1926), *The Cat and the Canary* (1927), *The Last Warning* (1929), and *Show Boat* (1929). **Rod La Rocque**, see entry No. 28. **286. Stan Laurel** (1890–1965) and **Oliver Hardy** (1892–1957). A unique team brought together by Hal Roach in 1926 and active until 1950, these gentlemen comedians proved there was more to comedy than slapstick vulgarity. Films include *Duck Soup* (1927), *Love 'Em and Weep* (1927), *The Battle of the Century* (1927), *Flying Elephants* (1928), *From Soup to Nuts* (1928), *Two Tars* (1928), *Liberty* (1929), and *Big Business* (1929).

285

286

287

287. Florence Lawrence (1889–1938). She was the screen's first star, the original "Biograph Girl," who entered films in 1907 and chose suicide to end a career that consisted of extra work by the thirties. Films include *The Curtain Pole* (1909), *Resurrection* (1909), *The Awakening of Bess* (1909), *The Little Rebel* (1911), *Elusive Isabel* (1916), *The Unfoldment* (1922), and *The Greater Glory* (1926).   **288. Rex Lease** (1903–1966). Best known for talkie Westerns, but initially, he was a star of "B" silents. Films include *A Woman Who Sinned* (1924), *Before Midnight* (1925), *The Last Alarm* (1926), *The College Hero* (1927), and *Queen of the Chorus* (1928).

288

289

290

289. Gwen Lee (1904–1961). Lanky, blonde, wisecracking sidekick both in silents and talkies; a perfect foil for any star. Films include *Pretty Ladies* (1925), *Upstage* (1926), *Orchids and Ermine* (1927), *Laugh, Clown, Laugh* (1928), and *Show Girl* (1928). **290. Lila Lee** (1905–1973). After a vaudeville career with Gus Edwards, with whom she was known as "Cuddles," Lila Lee was signed to a Famous Players-Lasky contract in the late 'teens and groomed for stardom. She was active through 1937 and was married, at one time, to actor James Kirkwood. Films include *The Cruise of the Make-Believe* (1918; her first film), *Male and Female* (1919), *Hawthorne of the U. S. A.* (1919), *Midsummer Madness* (1920), *Blood and Sand* (1922), *Love's Whirlpool* (1924), and *The Adorable Cheat* (1928).

292

291

291. Robert Z. Leonard (1889–1968). Major M-G-M contract director of the twenties through fifties — *The Great Ziegfeld* (1936), *Pride and Prejudice* (1940), etc. — Leonard began his film career as an actor at Selig in 1907; while at Universal in the 'teens, he was leading man to Ella Hall and known as "The Blonde Giant of the Screen;" married to actresses Mae Murray and Gertrude Olmsted. Films include *The Still Alarm* (1911), *The Novice* (1911), *Robinson Crusoe* (1913), *The Primeval Test* (1914), *The Master Key* (1914), and *The Crippled Hand* (1916). **292. Gladys Leslie** (1899–1976). A Vitagraph leading lady from 1917–1920, Gladys Leslie was billed as "The Girl with the Million Dollar Smile." Films include *Ransom's Folly* (1915), *Betrayed* (1916), *His Own People* (1917), *Wild Primrose* (1918), *Too Many Crooks* (1919), *The Midnight Bride* (1920), *God's Country and the Law* (1921), *If Winter Comes* (1923), and *Enemies of Youth* (1925).

293

294

293. Ralph Lewis (1872–1937). A massive, dominating screen presence as Austin Stoneman in *The Birth of a Nation* (1915), Ralph Lewis began his screen career with D. W. Griffith in 1914 and was active through the thirties. Films include *The Great Leap* (1914), *Let Katy Do It* (1916), *The Children Pay* (1916), *Jack and the Beanstalk* (1917), *Eyes of Youth* (1920), *The Conquering Power* (1921), and *Dante's Inferno* (1924).

294. Sheldon Lewis (1869–1958). Noted for his strong characterizations, Sheldon Lewis played Dr. Jekyll and Mr. Hyde twice on screen: in 1920 and 1930. Films include *The House of Fear* (1915), *The Iron Claw* (1916), *Charity* (1916), *The Bishop's Emeralds* (1919), *Orphans of the Storm* (1921), *The Enemy Sex* (1925), *Accused* (1925), *Don Juan* (1926), *Burning Gold* (1927), and *Seven Footprints to Satan* (1929).

295

297

296

298

299

295. Vera Lewis (1873–1956). Because of her rather unpleasant demeanor as one of "The Uplifters" in *Intolerance* (1916), one tends to forget that Vera Lewis had the attractive features of a mature woman; married to actor Ralph Lewis and entered films with D. W. Griffith in 1914. Films include *Sunshine Molly* (1915), *Jack and the Beanstalk* (1917), *A Bit of Jade* (1918), *Lombardi, Ltd.* (1919), *The Poor Simp* (1920), *Peg o' My Heart* (1922), *Stella Dallas* (1925), and *Ella Cinders* (1926). **296. Max Linder** (1883–1925). Charlie Chaplin acknowledged his debt to Linder and historian Jack Spears called him, "The motion picture's first great comedian, and its first genuine star." He began his screen career in France in 1905 and made his U. S. debut with Essanay in 1917. Films include *Max Comes Across* (1917; his first U. S. film), *Max Wants a Divorce* (1917), *Max and His Taxi* (1917), *Seven Years Bad Luck* (1921), *Be My Wife* (1921), and *The Three Must-Get-Theres* (1922). **297. Ann Little** (1894–1984). Active through 1923, Ann Little began her career with Thomas H. Ince in 1911 and was later under contract to Paramount. A reliable leading lady often playing opposite Wallace Reid, she later managed the Chateau Marmont Hotel in West Hollywood. Films include *The Land o' Lizards* (1916), *Nan of Music Mountain* (1917), *The World for Sale* (1918), *The Squaw Man* (1918), *The Roaring Road* (1919), *Square Deal Sanderson* (1919), and *Hair Trigger Casey* (1922). **298. Lucien Littlefield** (1895–1960). On screen from 1914 through 1958, Lucien Littlefield was excellent in characterizations of harrassed fathers, most notably Mary Pickford's in *My Best Girl* (1927). Films include *The Warrens of Virginia* (1915), *The Hostage* (1917), *Jack Straw* (1920), *The Sheik* (1921), *Manslaughter* (1922), *Babbitt* (1924), *Tumbleweeds* (1925), and *The Cat and the Canary* (1927).
299. Harold Lloyd (1893–1971). Harold Lloyd was the great, unassuming silent screen comedian whose glasses were his trademark and whose films are still a joy to watch. He entered films in 1912 and came to fame under the guidance of Hal Roach, from whom he broke away in 1923. He continued as a major comedy star through the late forties. Films include *Bumping Into Broadway* (1919), *Grandma's Boy* (1922), *Safety Last* (1923), *Girl Shy* (1924), *The Freshman* (1925), *For Heaven's Sake* (1926), *The Kid Brother* (1927), and *Speedy* (1928). Autobiography: *An American Comedy* (New York: Longmans, Green, 1928).

300

301

300. Harold Lockwood (1887–1918). One of the screen's first matinée idols, Harold Lockwood was in films from 1911 and co-starred in more than twenty features with May Allison between 1915 and 1917. He was a victim of the Spanish influenza epidemic. Films include *The Deserter* (1912), *Hearts Adrift* (1914), *Tess of the Storm Country* (1914), *Such a Little Queen* (1914), *Wildflower* (1914), *David Harum* (1915), *The Haunted Pajamas* (1917), *Broadway Bill* (1918), and *A Man of Honor* (1919; his last film).

301. Jacqueline Logan (1902–1983). A Ziegfeld *Follies* beauty who entered films in 1920. After her performance as Mary Magdalene in *The King of Kings* (1927), Jacqueline Logan seemed destined to portray "bad girls with good intentions." Films include *The Perfect Crime* (1920; her first film), *Molly O'* (1921), *Java Head* (1923), and *Midnight Madness* (1928).

302

303

302. Walter Long (1879–1952). The greatest of all silent screen villains, giving an unsurpassed performance as Gus in *The Birth of a Nation* (1915). Walter Long's career in films lasted from 1909 through 1950, during which time he menaced everyone from Mary Pickford to Rudolph Valentino. Films include *Martyrs of the Alamo* (1915), *Let Katy Do It* (1916), *The Little American* (1917), *Scarlet Days* (1919), *The Sheik* (1921), *Moran of the Lady Letty* (1922), *The Road to Yesterday* (1925), and *The Yankee Clipper* (1927).

303. Bessie Love (1898-1986). A D. W. Griffith discovery who began her career with *Intolerance* (1916), Bessie Love matured from a petite silent ingénue to one of the screen's major stars of early musicals such as *Broadway Melody* (1929) and *Chasing Rainbows* (1930). Films include *The Flying Torpedo* (1916), *The Aryan* (1916), *A Fighting Colleen* (1919), *The Sea Lion* (1921), *Human Wreckage* (1923), *The Lost World* (1925), *Soul Fire* (1925), and more than thirty sound features. Autobiography: *From Hollywood with Love* (London: Elm Tree Books, 1977).

304

304. Montagu Love (1877–1943). A classic screen villain who made more than 160 films between 1914 and 1946, Montagu Love's acting potential is obvious from his performance opposite Lillian Gish in *The Wind* (1928). Films include *Hearts in Exile* (1915; his first film), *Rasputin, The Black Monk* (1917), *The Volunteer* (1918), *The Riddle: Woman* (1920), *Forever* (1921), *The Eternal City* (1923), *The Son of the Sheik* (1926), *Don Juan* (1926), and *The King of Kings* (1927). He appears in this photograph with wrestler Kontsonaros.

305

305. Louise Lovely (1897–1980). Louise Lovely entered films in her native Australia before coming to Hollywood and joining Universal in 1915. It was claimed that the studio created her name because she was such "a lovely lady." Films include *Father and the Boys* (1915), *The Field of Honor* (1917), *The Butterfly Man* (1920), *Life's Greatest Question* (1921), and *Shattered Idols* (1922).   **306. Edmund Lowe** (1890–1971) and **Victor McLaglen** (1886–1959). These two men were first paired together as Sergeant Quirk and Captain Flagg in *What Price Glory* (1926), which led to a series of features. Edmund Lowe was on screen from the late 'teens. Victor McLaglen was discovered in British films by J. Stuart Blackton and specialized in tough, yet kindly characters (often Irish) in the films of John Ford. Lowe's films include *Eyes of Youth* (1919), *Peacock Alley* (1922), *The White Flower* (1923), *Barbara Frietchie* (1924), *East Lynne* (1925), and *Is Zat So?* (1927). McLaglen's films include *The Beloved Brute* (1924; his first U. S. film), *The Fighting Heart* (1925), *Beau Geste* (1926), *Loves of Carmen* (1927), and *Hangman's House* (1928).

306

307

308

307. Wilfred Lucas (1871–1940). In appearance, not a typical leading man, but by all accounts, one of the better dramatic actors of 'teens features who also directed. His career as a star (begun in 1908) came to a standstill in the twenties. Films include *Enoch Arden* (1911), *Man's Genesis* (1912), *The Massacre* (1912), *The Lily and the Rose* (1916), *Acquitted* (1916), *Jim Bludso* (1917), *Soldiers of Fortune* (1919), *Trilby* (1923), and *Dorothy Vernon of Haddon Hall* (1924).

308. Ben Lyon (1901–1979). Ben Lyon was an unpretentious, easy-going actor who was equally at home in silent films or on British radio with his first wife, actress Bebe Daniels, as the stars of *Life With the Lyons* (1950–1961). One of his earliest films, *Open Your Eyes* (1919), was on the dangers of venereal disease, and after that inauspicious start, it was three years before he became a featured leading man. Films include *The Heart of Maryland* (1921), *So Big* (1924), *The Perfect Sap* (1927), *Hell's Angels* (1930), *Indiscreet* (1931), *I Cover the Waterfront* (1933), and *The Lyons in Paris* (1954; his last film). Autobiography: *Life with the Lyons* (London: Odhams, 1953).

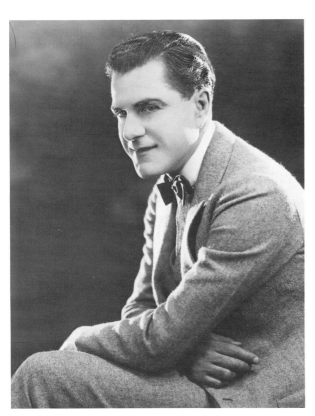

309

310

309. Bert Lytell (1885–1954). A popular actor of stage, screen, radio, and television, Bert Lytell began his screen career in 1917 and was often cast opposite Alice Lake. Films include *Alias Jimmy Valentine* (1920), *The Right of Way* (1920), *A Message From Mars* (1921), *The Eternal City* (1923), *Lady Windermere's Fan* (1925), and *The Gilded Butterfly* (1926).

310. Marc MacDermott (1881–1929). After joining Edison in 1908 and becoming the company's leading male star, Marc MacDermott developed into a fine character player as exemplified by his triple roles in *While New York Sleeps* (1920). Films include *The Passer-By* (1912), *Eugene Aram* (1915), *Kathleen Mavourneen* (1919), *The Spanish Jade* (1922), *He Who Gets Slapped* (1924), *The Goose Woman* (1925), *Flesh and the Devil* (1926), and *Glorious Betsy* (1928).

311

311. Katherine MacDonald (1891–1956). A medio-cre actress but so attractive that she was known as "The American Beauty." Katherine MacDonald feuded with her sister, Mary MacLaren, and was rumored to be the mistress of Woodrow Wilson. Films include *Battling Jane* (1918), *The Squaw Man* (1918), *The Beauty Market* (1919), *The Turning Point* (1920), *The Beautiful Liar* (1921), *The Infidel* (1922), *Chastity* (1923), and *Old Loves and New* (1926). She appears in this photograph with actor Roy Stewart.

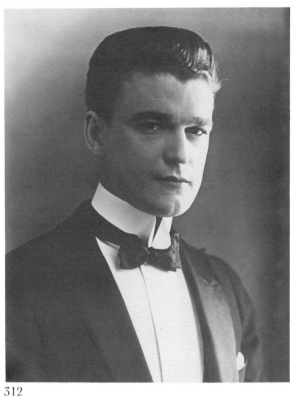

312

313

312. Wallace MacDonald (1891–1978). *Motion Picture Classic* (September 1921) noted Wallace MacDonald's "straight-backed, manly heroism which one often finds in the Frank Merriwell stories." Married to actress Doris May, he later produced "B" pictures and was well liked in the industry. Films include *Purity* (1916), *Mlle. Paulette* (1918), *Leave It To Susan* (1919), *Trumpet Island* (1920), *A Fool There Was* (1922), *The Spoilers* (1923), *Pampered Youth* (1925), and *Drums of the Desert* (1927).

313. Fred Mace (????–1917). An original member of Mack Sennett's Keystone Company, Fred Mace began his career at American Biograph in 1911 and ended it possibly in suicide. Films include *The Diving Girl* (1911), *One-Round O'Brien* (1912), *Without Hope* (1914), *My Valet* (1915), *Crooked to the End* (1915), *His Last Scent* (1916), and *A Village Vampire* (1916).

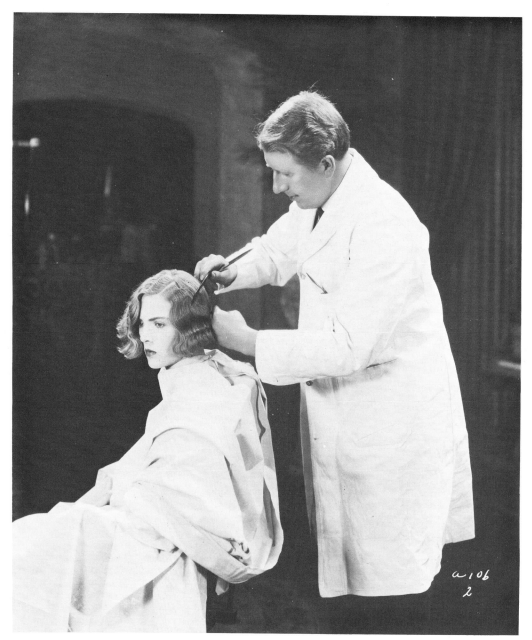

314

314. Dorothy Mackaill (1903–). In a career that lasted from 1921–1937, Dorothy Mackaill was equally at ease as a breezy comedienne (in the "Torchy" series opposite Johnny Hines) or a semi-tragedienne. "She loses her own personality directly she dons the clothes of the film character she is creating," wrote *Picturegoer* (August 1926). Despite her apparent American sophistication, she was born in the far-from-glamorous North British city of Hull. Films include *The Fighting Blade* (1923), *Chickie* (1925), *Shore Leave* (1925), and *The Whip* (1928). She appears in this photograph having her hair styled by Charles of the Ritz.

315

316

317

315. Douglas MacLean (1890–1967). One of the better light comedians of the twenties who came to prominence under contract to Thomas Ince, Douglas MacLean later became a producer. Films include *The Hun Within* (1918), *Johanna Enlists* (1918), *Captain Kidd, Jr.* (1919), *25-½ Hours Leave* (1920), *The Home Stretch* (1921), *The Hottentot* (1922), and *Seven Keys to Baldpate* (1925). **316. Mary MacLaren** (1896–1985). Mary MacLaren entered films in 1916 with Universal under Lois Weber's direction. She enjoyed a career as a leading lady until 1924, but ended her days in poverty and the subject of much publicity. She was the sister of Katherine MacDonald. Films include *Shoes* (1916), *The Mysterious Mrs. M.* (1917), *The Unpainted Woman* (1919), *The Three Musketeers* (1921), *Outcast* (1922), *Under the Red Robe* (1923), and *The Uninvited Guest* (1924). **317. Cleo Madison** (1883–1964). A major Universal contract star of the mid-'teens and also a director with the studio, Cleo Madison was active from 1913 through 1924. Films include *The Trey o' Hearts* (1914 serial), *The Chalice of Sorrow* (1916), *Black Orchids* (1917), *The Romance of Tarzan* (1918), *The Girl From Nowhere* (1919), *The Lure of Youth* (1921), and *Souls in Bondage* (1923).

319

318

318. Martha Mansfield (1900–1923). Photographer Alfred Cheney Johnston described Martha Mansfield as "an exquisite pastel — a fragile flower." She died when her dress caught fire while filming *The Warrens of Virginia* (1923). Films include *Broadway Bill* (1918), *Civilian Clothes* (1920), *Till We Meet Again* (1922), *Potash and Perlmutter* (1923), and *Youthful Cheaters* (1923). **319. George Marion** (1860–1945). A character actor indifferent to his screen career, George Marion recreated his original stage role of Chris in the 1923 and 1930 film versions of Eugene O'Neill's *Anna Christie*. Films include *Go Straight* (1921), *Tumbleweeds* (1925), *The King of Kings* (1927), and *Evangeline* (1929). **320. Enid Markey** (1891–1981). A major Thomas Ince star of the mid-'teens, Enid Markey went on to become the screen's first Jane in *Tarzan of the Apes* (1918). She interspersed a stage career with film appearances through *The Boston Strangler* (1968). Films include *Between Men* (1915), *The Iron Strain* (1915), *Civilization* (1916), and *Foolish Mothers* (1923).

321

321. June Marlowe (1903–1984). An unobtrusive actress ideally suited to supporting Rin-Tin-Tin, Our Gang, and various comedians in the thirties. Films include *Find Your Man* (1924), *Clash of the Wolves* (1925), *Don Juan* (1926), *The Life of Riley* (1927), and *Alias the Deacon* (1928).

322

323

322. Percy Marmont (1883–1977). On stage from the late 1890's, English-born Percy Marmont entered American films in 1918, becoming a somewhat harried-looking leading man. Later, he became a fine British character actor in sound features. Films include *Rose of the World* (1918; his first U. S. film), *Vengeance of Durand* (1919), *The Sporting Duchess* (1920), *If Winter Comes* (1923), *The Light That Failed* (1923), *Lord Jim* (1925), *Aloma of the South Seas* (1926), and *Mantrap* (1926).

323. Mae Marsh (1895–1968). Without question, the greatest dramatic actress of the silent era, thanks to her roles in *The Birth of a Nation* (1915) and *Intolerance* (1916), Mae Marsh was a D. W. Griffith discovery who failed to live up to expectations in the films of other directors. She entered films with the American Biograph Company in 1912, and was under contract to Goldwyn from 1916–1919 and Robertson-Cole in 1920. Films include *Man's Genesis* (1912), *The Escape* (1914), *Hoodoo Ann* (1916), *Polly of the Circus* (1917), *The White Rose* (1923), *The Rat* (1925), *Over the Hill* (1932), and extra work for the next thirty years.

324

325

325. Shirley Mason (1901–1979). The younger sister of actress Viola Dana, Shirley Mason made her screen debut in 1910 and continued to star through the next nineteen years in more than ninety films. Films include *Children Who Labor* (1912), *Vanity Fair* (1915), *Treasure Island* (1920), and *Lord Jim* (1925).

324. Tully Marshall (1864–1943). Tully Marshall's presence in a film always boded well for the audience and for the production. His favorite role was as Bridger in *The Covered Wagon* (1923), but he was at his best as Baron Sadoja in *The Merry Widow* (1925). Films include *Paid in Full* (1914; his first film), *The Devil's Needle* (1916), *Oliver Twist* (1916), *M'Liss* (1918), *Hail the Woman* (1921), *The Hunchback of Notre Dame* (1923), *The Cat and the Canary* (1927), *Ball of Fire* (1941), and *Behind Prison Bars* (1943; his last film).

326

326. Mrs. Mary Maurice (1844–1918). The first actress to gain fame as the perfect screen mother, Mary Maurice was with Vitagraph from 1910 almost until her death. Films include *My Old Dutch* (1911), *The Seventh Son* (1912), *The Sins of the Mothers* (1914), *The Battle Cry of Peace* (1915), *The Goddess* (1915), and *Rose of the South* (1916). **327. Ken Maynard** (1895–1973). Ken Maynard was a cowboy star who was very popular with the Saturday matinée crowd and made up in action for what he lacked in sophistication; on screen from 1923 through 1970. Films include *$50,000 Reward* (1924), *North Star* (1925), *The Haunted Range* (1926), *The Overland Stage* (1927), *The Upland Rider* (1928), and *California Mail* (1929).

327

328

329

328. Frank Mayo (1889–1963). Frank Mayo was a competent actor on stage and screen, beginning his career with Selig. He introduced his wife, Dagmar Godowsky, to films (for which, perhaps, he should not be forgiven). Films include *Betsy Ross* (1917), *The Purple Lily* (1918), *Lasca* (1919), *The Marriage Pit* (1920), *Go Straight* (1921), *Souls for Sale* (1923), *Passionate Youth* (1925), and *Then Came the Woman* (1926). **329. May McAvoy** (1901–1984). May McAvoy began her career as an extra at Fox in 1917 and was signed to a Paramount starring contract in 1921. Her role as Al Jolson's leading lady in *The Jazz Singer* (1927) has overshadowed her excellent work in many major silent features. Films include *Sentimental Tommy* (1921), *The Enchanted Cottage* (1924), *Lady Windermere's Fan* (1925), and *Ben-Hur* (1926). **330. Claire McDowell** (1877–1966). A mature-looking actress who joined the American Biograph Company and D. W. Griffith in 1910 and remained with the Company through the mid-'teens, Claire McDowell became a busy supporting actress in twenties features. She married fellow Biograph actor Charles Hill Mailes. Films include *The Female of the Species* (1912), *Midsummer Madness* (1920), *Quincy Adams Sawyer* (1922), *Human Wreckage* (1923), *Secrets* (1924), *Four Devils* (1929), and *The Viking* (1929).

330

332

331

331. J. P. McGowan (1880–1952). More a director (including *The Hazards of Helen* serial with his wife, Helen Holmes) than an actor, J. P. McGowan specialized in action roles. According to Terry Ramsaye, he became an actor "because he could shoot a rabbit on the run from the back of a galloping horse." Films include *Seth's Temptation* (1910; his first film), *Poacher's Pardon* (1912), *From the Manger to the Cross* (1912), and *The Eighth Notch* (1913).   **332. Malcolm McGregor** (1892–1945). Hailed as the twenties' answer to Wallace Reid, Malcolm McGregor was an extra before director Rex Ingram featured him in *The Prisoner of Zenda* (1922). Films include *Smouldering Fires* (1925), *The Circle* (1925), *Don Juan's Three Nights* (1926), and *Buck Privates* (1928).

333

334

333. Raymond McKee (1892–1984). Raymond McKee's stage debut was at three years of age, and his film debut in 1911. He is memorable in *Down to the Sea in Ships* (1922). Films include *The Heart of the Hills* (1916), *The Apple-Tree Girl* (1917), *Kathleen Mavourneen* (1919), *Flame of Youth* (1920), *Babbitt* (1924), *The Speed Limit* (1926), and *Heart to Heart* (1928). **Victor McLaglen**, see entry No. 306. **Lucille McVey**, see entry No. 154.

334. Thomas Meighan (1879–1936). A typical strong, rugged leading man, Thomas Meighan was under contract to Paramount from 1915–1928. Films include *Kindling* (1915), *The Trail of the Lonesome Pine* (1916), *M'Liss* (1918), *The Miracle Man* (1919), *Male and Female* (1919), *Manslaughter* (1922), *The Alaskan* (1924), *The Canadian* (1926), *The Racket* (1928), and *Peck's Bad Boy* (1934; his last film).

335

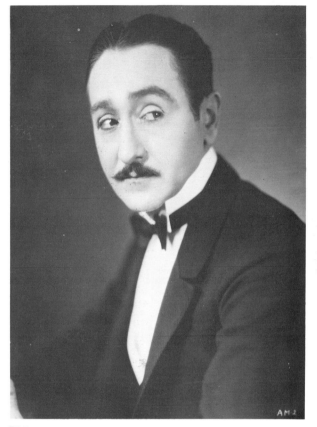

336

335. George Melford (1877–1961). A competent director best known for Rudolph Valentino's *The Sheik* (1921), George Melford began his screen career as an actor at Kalem from 1909 through 1914. Later, he turned to directing and ended his career as a bit player in 1953. Films include *The Wayward Daughter* (1909; his first film), *The Usurer* (1913), and *The Barrier of Ignorance* (1914).

336. Adolphe Menjou (1890–1963). A model of suave urbanity in silents and talkies, Adolphe Menjou was at his best in *A Woman of Paris* (1923). Unfortunately, Menjou's urbanity did not stretch to his politics, which were vindictively right-wing. Films include *The Three Musketeers* (1921), *The Sheik* (1921), *The Spanish Dancer* (1923), *The Marriage Circle* (1924), *Are Parents People?* (1925), *The Sorrows of Satan* (1926), and more than sixty sound films over the next three decades. Autobiography: *It Took Nine Tailors* (New York: Whittlesey, 1948).

337

339

338

337. Charlotte Merriam (1906–1972). One of the last contract leading ladies at Vitagraph, Charlotte Merriam was later featured in Christie comedies. Films include *The Brass Bottle* (1923), *Captain Blood* (1924), *Pampered Youth* (1925), and *The Candy Kid* (1928). **338. Violet Mersereau** (1897–????). Child actress of the stage who became a Universal IMP star in 1914, Violet Mersereau was billed as "The Child Wonder." Films include *The Spitfire* (1914), *The Avalanche* (1915), *Broken Fetters* (1916), *Little Miss Nobody* (1917), *The Nature Girl* (1919), *Nero* (1922), *Luck* (1923), and *Lend Me Your Husband* (1924). **339. Beatriz Michelena** (1890–1942). Noted for her characterizations of Bret Harte heroines for the California Motion Picture Corporation. Films include *Mrs. Wiggs of the Cabbage Patch* (1914), *Salomy Jane* (1915), *The Unwritten Law* (1916), *The Heart of Juanita* (1919), and *The Flame of Hellgate* (1920).

340

341

340. Patsy Ruth Miller (1905–). After several years as an extra and "bit" player, Patsy Ruth Miller came to fame as Esmeralda in *The Hunchback of Notre Dame* (1923). Films include *The Sheik* (1921), *Omar The Tentmaker* (1922), *The Yankee Consul* (1924), *So This is Paris* (1926), and *What Every Girl Should Know* (1927). **Autobiography:** *My Hollywood — When Both of Us Were Young* (Brigantine, NJ: O'Raghailligh, 1988). **341. Walter Miller** (1892–1940). Walter Miller was an excellent leading man at American Biograph from 1912, whose later action features and serials were never equal to his talents. Films include *Oil and Water* (1912), *The Mothering Heart* (1913), *The Toll of Justice* (1916), *Miss Robinson Crusoe* (1917), *Thin Ice* (1919), *Unconquered Woman* (1922), *Playthings of Desire* (1924), and *The Unfair Sex* (1926).

342. Alyce Mills (–). A minor career as a leading lady from 1923 through 1927. Films include *A Bride for a Knight* (1923), *Daughters of the Night* (1924), *The Keeper of the Bees* (1925), *The Prince of Broadway* (1926), and *The Whirlwind of Youth* (1927).   **343. Mary Miles Minter** (1902–1984). Despite a career that lasted from 1915–1923, Mary Miles Minter was little more than a pretty face masking an inability to act. She became a Metro contract star in 1915 after two earlier films and was a Realart/Paramount star from 1919–1923. Her association with director William Desmond Taylor, whose 1922 murder is usually attributed to Minter's mother, Charlotte Shelby, ended her career. Films include *Barbara Frietchie* (1915), *Dimples* (1916), *The Ghost of Rosie Taylor* (1918), *Anne of Green Gables* (1919), and *The Trail of the Lonesome Pine* (1923; her last film).   **344. Rhea Mitchell** (1893–1957). A petite, blonde actress who began her career with the New York Motion Picture Company in the early 'teens. Films include *The Brink* (1915), *D'Artagnan* (1916), *The Goat* (1918), *The Money Corral* (1919), *Good Women* (1921), *The Greatest Menace* (1923), *The Other Kind of Love* (1924), and *Modern Youth* (1926).

343

342

344

345

345. Tom Mix (1880–1940). The best known and most glamorous of all silent Western stars, Tom Mix's Fox features (1918–1927) are still great fun, thanks to Mix's style and use of fast-paced action. Mix entered films with Selig in 1910 and remained on screen through the mid-thirties. Films include *Ranch Life in the Great Southwest* (1910), *Sage Brush Tom* (1915), *The Heart of Texas Ryan* (1917), *Trailin'* (1921), *Just Tony* (1922), *Riders of the Purple Sage* (1925), and *The Great K and A Train Robbery* (1926). He appears in this photograph with his horse, Tony.

346

346. Baby Peggy Montgomery (1918–). The female answer to Jackie Coogan, Baby Peggy Montgomery has become known in more recent years as Diana Serra Cary, the author of two books on Hollywood history. Films include *The Darling of New York* (1923), *Captain January* (1924), *April Fool* (1926), *Sensation Seekers* (1927), and *West of Santa Fe* (1928).

347. Colleen Moore (1902–1988) and **Antonio Moreno** (1886–1967). Bobbed hair and talent best described Colleen Moore; she was a major silent star who was superb in one of her last talkies: *The Power and the Glory* (1933). Films include *Bad Boy* (1917; her first film), *Little Orphant Annie* (1918), *Dinty* (1920), *Flaming Youth* (1923), *So Big* (1924), *Sally* (1925), *Ella Cinders* (1926), *Orchids and Ermine* (1927), *Lilac Time* (1928), and *The Scarlet Letter* (1934; her last film). Autobiography: *Silent Star* (Garden City, NY: Doubleday, 1968). Antonio Moreno was perhaps the screen's first Latin Lover and certainly one of the better actors in that category. Films include *Under False Colors* (1914), *The Island of Regeneration* (1915), *The Trail of the Lonesome Pine* (1923), *The Spanish Dancer* (1923), *Mare Nostrum* (1926), *Beverly of Graustark* (1926), *The Temptress* (1926), and *It* (1927).

347

348

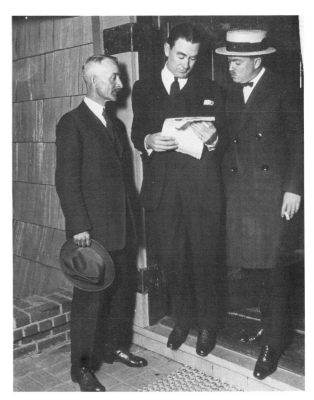

349

350

351

352

348. Matt Moore (1888–1960). The most youthful looking of the Moore brothers, Matt began his screen career at Universal in 1913. He remained active as a major star through the twenties and was a featured player into the fifties. Films include *Traffic in Souls* (1913), *20,000 Leagues Under the Sea* (1916), *The Pride of the Clan* (1917), *The Unpardonable Sin* (1919), *Back Pay* (1922), *The Unholy Three* (1925), *His Majesty, Bunker Bean* (1925), and *Diplomacy* (1926).   **349. Owen Moore** (1886–1939). The first husband of Mary Pickford (1911–1920) and the brother of Matt and Tom Moore, Owen Moore entered films with D. W. Griffith in 1908 and was active through 1937. Films include *The Battle of the Sexes* (1914), *Home, Sweet Home* (1914), *Mistress Nell* (1915), *Piccadilly Jim* (1920), *The Chicken in the Case* (1921), *Torment* (1924), *The Red Mill* (1927), and *She Done Him Wrong* (1933). In this photograph he is receiving his divorce papers from Mary Pickford while director/screenwriter Victor Heerman (in straw hat) looks on.   **350. Tom Moore** (1883–1955). Beginning his career with American Biograph in 1908, Tom Moore was on screen through 1950 as a dependable, somewhat wooden leading man.

He was prominent at Kalem from 1912 through 1915. Films include *The Prodigal* (1914), *The Cinderella Man* (1917), *Brown of Harvard* (1918), *The Gay Lord Quex* (1919), *Officer 666* (1920), *Mr. Barnes of New York* (1922), *Manhandled* (1924), and *A Kiss for Cinderella* (1926). Tom Moore is on the left; in the foreground is director Charles Giblyn.   **351. Victor Moore** (1876–1962). A prominent stage and vaudeville performer, Victor Moore came to the screen with Famous Players-Lasky as the character Chimmie Fadden. He enjoyed greater success in talkies, most notably as Barkley Cooper in *Make Way for Tomorrow* (1937). Films include *Chimmie Fadden* (1915), *Chimmie Fadden Out West* (1915), *Snobs* (1915), *The Clown* (1916), *The Race* (1916), and *The Man Who Found Himself* (1925).   **352. Lois Moran** (1908–). Lois Moran, commented *Photoplay*, had "a suggestion of poised and well mannered youth." This was certainly true of her first American screen role in *Stella Dallas* (1925) and for the remainder of her film career through 1931. Films include *The Road to Mandalay* (1926), *The Music Master* (1927), *Love Hungry* (1928), and *Mammy* (1930). **Antonio Moreno**, see entry No. 347.

354

353

353. Harry T. Morey (1873–1936). A Vitagraph leading man of the 'teens whose career petered out in the twenties. Films include *My Official Wife* (1914), *Crooky* (1915), *Whom the Gods Destroy* (1916), *Within the Law* (1917), *Tangled Lives* (1918), *The Birth of a Soul* (1920), *The Curse of Drink* (1922), and *Captain January* (1924). **354. James Morrison** (1888–1974). A perennial juvenile at Vitagraph from 1910–1916 and, later, on a freelance basis. James Morrison retired from the screen in 1925. Films include *The Christian* (1914), *The Battle Cry of Peace* (1915), *The Enemy* (1916), *Womanhood, The Glory of a Nation* (1917), *Over the Top* (1918), *Black Beauty* (1921), *The Little Minister* (1922), and *Captain Blood* (1924).

355

356

355. Charles Morton (1908–1966). A "pretty" leading man of late silents under contract to Fox. Films include *Colleen* (1927), *Four Sons* (1928), *Four Devils* (1929), and *Christina* (1929).   **356. Marie Mosquini** (1899–1983). A secretary in 1916 to Hal Roach who became a fine female support to Will Rogers, Charley Chase, and Snub Pollard in the twenties. Films include *Big Game* (1921), *At the Ringside* (1921), *Sold at Auction* (1923), *Hustling Hank* (1923), *Uncensored Movies* (1923), *Going to Congress* (1924), *Gee Whiz, Genevieve* (1924), *Good and Naughty* (1926), and *7th Heaven* (1927).   **357. Jack Mulhall** (1887–1979). An amiable leading man with a beguiling smile, Jack Mulhall began his screen career in 1914 and ended his days as a character player and field representative for the Screen Actors Guild. By 1938, he claimed to have appeared in more than 1,000 films. Films include *Madame Spy* (1917), *All of a Sudden Peggy* (1920), *Molly O'* (1921), *Turn to the Right* (1922), *God Gave Me Twenty Cents* (1926), *Orchids and Ermine* (1927), and *Smile, Brother, Smile* (1927).

357

358

359

358. Edna Murphy (1899–1974). One-time wife of Mervyn LeRoy, Edna Murphy was on screen from 1919 through 1932, developing from an ingénue to a flapper. Films include *Live Wires* (1921), *Nobody's Bride* (1923), *Into the Net* (1924), *The White Moth* (1924), *Lena Rivers* (1925), *College Days* (1926), and *Modern Daughters* (1927).   **359. Charles Murray** (1872–1941). Charles Murray was a rubber-faced comedian who usually suffered at the hands of domineering women. He was on screen from 1911 and at his best in the "Cohen and Kelly" series of comedy features. Films include *Yankee Doodle in Berlin* (1919), *A Small Town Idol* (1921), *Lilies of the Field* (1924), *The Wizard of Oz* (1925), *The Cohens and Kellys* (1926), and *McFadden's Flats* (1927).   **360. Mae Murray** (1889–1965). A star whose personality was greater than her acting ability, Mae Murray's bee-stung lips were her trademark in a career that lasted from 1916–1931. She gained prominence on stage in the 1908 Ziegfeld *Follies* and was under contract to Famous Players/Paramount from 1916–1917, Universal from 1917–1919, and Metro/M-G-M from 1922–1927. Films include *Sweet Kitty Bellairs* (1916), *The Mormon Maid* (1917), *Princess Virtue* (1917), *Peacock Alley* (1922), and *The Merry Widow* (1925). Autobiography: *The Self-Enchanted* (New York: McGraw-Hill, 1959).

MM-47

361

361. Carmel Myers (1901–1980). Thanks to her penchant for publicity, Carmel Myers' career has become somewhat more important than it actually was. A competent actress but no more than that, Miss Myers was in films, on and off, from 1916 through 1976. Films include *A Love Sublime* (1917), *Sirens of the Sea* (1917), *A Society Sensation* (1918), *Babbitt* (1924), *Beau Brummell* (1924), *Ben-Hur* (1926), *Tell It to the Marines* (1926), and *Sorrell and Son* (1927).

363

Yours faithfully
Harry C. Myers

362

362. Harry C. Myers (1882–1938). A portly leading man, memorable as the drunken millionaire in Chaplin's *City Lights* (1931), Harry C. Myers was an important star with the Lubin Company in the early 'teens. Films include *The Earl of Pawtucket* (1915), *Out of the Night* (1918), *A Connecticut Yankee at King Arthur's Court* (1920), *Turn to the Right* (1922), *Little Johnny Jones* (1923), *Zander the Great* (1925), *Exit Smiling* (1926), and *The Dove* (1927).   **363. Conrad Nagel** (1897–1970). An insipid, yet busy actor on stage, screen, radio, and television, Conrad Nagel was also a co-founder and president of The Academy of Motion Picture Arts and Sciences, and a leading spokesman for Actors' Equity. Films include *Little Women* (1919; his first film), *Midsummer Madness* (1920), *Grumpy* (1923), *Bella Donna* (1923), *Three Weeks* (1924), *Tess of the D'Urbervilles* (1924), *Sun Up* (1925), *The Exquisite Sinner* (1926), *Quality Street* (1927), *Glorious Betsy* (1928), and *The Man Who Understood Women* (1959; his last film).

364

365

364. Nita Naldi (1897–1961). A ludicrous vamp of twenties features, Nita Naldi was at her worst (or best) opposite Rudolph Valentino in *Blood and Sand* (1922). Films include *Dr. Jekyll and Mr. Hyde* (1920), *The Ten Commandments* (1923), *A Sainted Devil* (1924), *Cobra* (1925), *The Miracle of Life* (1926), and *What Price Beauty* (1928).

365. Betty Nansen (1873–1943). A celebrated Danish stage and screen actress, Betty Nansen arrived in the United States to star for Fox at the end of 1914 and returned to her native country a year later. Films include *A Woman of Impulse* (1915), *For Her Son* (1915), *A Woman's Resurrection* (1915), *Anna Karenina* (1915), and *The Celebrated Scandal* (1915).

THE BRAT.

366

366. Alla Nazimova (1879–1945). A brilliant stage actress whose film career failed to do her justice. Films include *War Brides* (1916; her first film), *Revelation* (1918), *The Red Lantern* (1919), *The Brat* (1919), *Camille* (1921), *Salome* (1923), *Blood and Sand* (1941), and *Since You Went Away* (1944; her last film).

367

368

369

367. Pola Negri (1894–1987). Polish-born Pola Negri came to the United States in 1922 as a result of her popularity in German films. Immediately, she became one of this country's leading dramatic stars, a veritable Queen of Tragedy, who became embroiled in a celebrated, publicity-oriented feud with the other top star on the Paramount lot, Gloria Swanson. Films include *Bella Donna* (1923; her first U. S. film), *The Cheat* (1923), *Woman of the World* (1925), *Hotel Imperial* (1927), *Barbed Wire* (1927), and *The Moon Spinners* (1964; her last film). Autobiography: *Memoirs of a Star* (Garden City, NY: Doubleday, 1970). **368. Miriam Nesbitt** (1873–1954). An important Edison star of the 'teens, Miriam Nesbitt twice travelled to England — in 1912 and 1913 — to appear in Edison productions there. Films include *The Passer-By* (1912), *Children Who Labor* (1912), *Mary Stuart* (1913), *The Way Back* (1915), *The Catspaw* (1916), and *Infidelity* (1917).

369. Anna Q. Nilsson (1888–1974). Sweden's first major contribution to the American cinema was Anna Q. Nilsson, a talented blonde in films from 1911 through 1950. Films include *The Regeneration* (1915), *Seven Keys to Baldpate* (1917), *The Toll Gate* (1920), *Adam's Rib* (1923), *Between Friends* (1924), *Sorrell and Son* (1927), and *The Whip* (1928).

370

371

370. Greta Nissen (1906–1988). Greta Nissen was a Norwegian-born beauty under contract to Paramount from 1925 through 1927, who was the original star of *Hell's Angels* (1930) but replaced by Jean Harlow when the film became a talkie. Films include *Lost — A Wife* (1925; her first film), *The King on Main Street* (1925), *The Wanderer* (1926), *The Love Thief* (1926), *Fazil* (1928), and *The Butter and Egg Man* (1928).

371. Marion/Marian Nixon (1904–1983). There is much truth to the comment from *Photoplay* magazine "Sometimes it is fatal to be too pretty. Marion Nixon goes on playing the little-girl-who-marries-the-hero, while less beautiful ladies get all the snappy roles." After her retirement from the screen, she married director William Seiter and, after his death, she married Ben Lyon. Films include *Riders of the Purple Sage* (1925), *Hands Up!* (1926), *Jazz Mad* (1928), *General Crack* (1929), *Rebecca of Sunnybrook Farm* (1932), and *Doctor Bull* (1933).   **372. Mabel Normand** (1894–1930). The best known of all silent comediennes and an attractive actress, but the majority of the extant Mabel Normand films seem to have lost their humorous appeal. After being a leading lady to and a director of Charlie Chaplin in the early 'teens, Mabel Normand went on to star for Mack Sennett and Sam Goldwyn. Films include *Mickey* (1918), *Peck's Bad Girl* (1918), *What Happened to Rosa?* (1921), *Molly O'* (1921), and *The Extra Girl* (1923).

373

374

373. Barry Norton (1909–1956). Active from the mid-twenties, Barry Norton was easily cast as a sensitive and romantic all-American, although he was actually Argentinian and later starred in and directed Spanish-language features. Films include *What Price Glory* (1926), *Sunrise — A Song of Two Humans* (1927), *Sins of the Fathers* (1928), and *Four Devils* (1929).
374. Eva Novak (1898–1988). She was not as talented as her older sister, Jane, but Eva Novak was a good, unobtrusive leading lady. Films include *The Feud* (1919), *The Testing Block* (1920), *The Torrent* (1921), *Chasing the Moon* (1922), *Boston Blackie* (1923), *Lure of the Yukon* (1924), *Sally* (1925), *Irene* (1926), and *Red Signals* (1927). **375. Jane Novak** (1895–). A demure actress who entered films in the early 'teens and was a leading lady to William S. Hart in five features: *The Tiger Man* (1918), *Selfish Yates* (1918), *The Money Corral* (1919), *Wagon Tracks* (1919), and *Three Word Brand* (1921). Films include *Behind the Door*

(1920), *The Rosary* (1922), *Lazybones* (1925), and *Redskin* (1929). **376. Ramon Novarro** (1899–1968). A rival to Rudolph Valentino and a far superior actor, Ramon Novarro began his screen career as an extra in 1917 — he was also working as a model — and became a star thanks to the efforts of director Rex Ingram in 1922. His homosexual-related murder was widely publicized. Films include *The Prisoner of Zenda* (1922), *Trifling Women* (1922), *Where the Pavement Ends* (1923), *Saramouche* (1923), *Ben-Hur* (1926), *The Student Prince in Old Heidelberg* (1927), *The Pagan* (1929), *Mata Hari* (1932), and *Heller in Pink Tights* (1960; his last film). **377. Laura Oakley** (1880–1957). A Universal actress of the early 'teens, Laura Oakley first starred there in "Nestor" and later, "Powers" brand comedies. Perhaps because of her build, she was named honorary fire chief of Universal City. Films include *Lord John in New York* (1915), *The Dumb Girl of Portici* (1916), and *Two-Gun Betty* (1918).

375

377

376

378

379

378. Wheeler Oakman (1890–1949). A Selig actor who appeared in the original production of *The Spoilers* (1914), Wheeler Oakman also uttered that immortal line heard for the first time on film in *Lights of New York* (1928): "Take him for a ride." Films include *The Rosary* (1915), *The Ne'er-Do-Well* (1916), *Princess Virtue* (1917), *Mickey* (1918), *The Virgin of Stamboul* (1920), *The Love Trap* (1923), and *In Borrowed Plumes* (1926).

379. Eugene O'Brien (1880–1966). A Broadway actor before he entered films in the mid-'teens, Eugene O'Brien is generally considered to have been at his best playing opposite Norma Talmadge. Films include *The Scarlet Woman* (1916), *The Moth* (1917), *Rebecca of Sunnybrook Farm* (1917), *Fires of Faith* (1919), *The Wonderful Chance* (1920), *Secrets* (1924), *Graustark* (1925), and *The Romantic Age* (1927).

380

380. George O'Brien (1900–1985). A much under-rated, sensitive silent actor, George O'Brien later displayed a naturalistic style of acting in his Fox sound Westerns that was unique among actors of this genre. Films include *The Iron Horse* (1924; his first film), *The Johnstown Flood* (1926), *Fig Leaves* (1926), *Sunrise — A Song of Two Humans* (1927), and *Noah's Ark* (1928).

382

381

381. Molly O'Day (–). A leading lady in Hal Roach comedies of the twenties, Molly O'Day was "discovered" by director Marshall Neilan. Films include *Hard-Boiled Haggerty* (1927), *The Patent Leather Kid* (1927), *The Shepherd of the Hills* (1928), and *The Little Shepherd of Kingdom Come* (1928). **382. Warner Oland** (1880–1938). Best known as the screen's Charlie Chan (from 1931 to his death), Warner Oland was particularly active in the silent era as a serial star: *Patria* (1917), *The Fatal Ring* (1917), *The Lightning Raider* (1919), etc. Films include *East Is West* (1922), *Don Q, Son of Zorro* (1925), *Don Juan* (1926), and *Old San Francisco* (1927).

384

383

383. Gertrude Olmsted/Olmstead (1897–1975). A nondescript leading lady of the twenties, married to director Robert Z. Leonard. Her career ended with the coming of sound. Films include *Cameo Kirby* (1923), *Babbitt* (1924), *Cobra* (1925), *California Straight Ahead* (1925), *Time, the Comedian* (1925), *The Torrent* (1926), and *Mr. Wu* (1927).   **384. Pat O'Malley** (1890–1966). Pat O'Malley was a competent leading man of silent films who started at Edison and later became a successful character actor in talkies. Films include *Bob Hampton of Placer* (1921), *My Wild Irish Rose* (1922), *Proud Flesh* (1925), and *My Old Dutch* (1926).

385

386

385. Baby Marie Osborne (1911–). The most important child star of the 'teens, by 1918, Marie Osborne had her own company; later, she became a stand-in and film costumer. Films include *Little Mary Sunshine* (1916; her first film), *Twin Kiddies* (1917), *The Child of M'sieu* (1919), and *The Little Diplomat* (1919).

386. Muriel Ostriche (1896–1989). "The Moxie Girl" (1915–1920), Muriel Ostriche enjoyed a film career from 1912–1921. Films include *A Tale of the Wilderness* (1912; her first film), *Lobster Salad and Milk* (1913), *All's Well That Ends Well* (1914), *Mortmain* (1915), *The Volunteer* (1917), and *The Sacred Flame* (1919).

387

387. Seena Owen (1894–1966). After entering films with Kalem in 1914, Seena Owen gained fame as Princess Beloved in *Intolerance* (1916). She was also memorable as another royal figure, Queen Regina V, in *Queen Kelly* (1928). Films include *The Fox Woman* (1915), *Branding Broadway* (1918), *Victory* (1919), *Lavender and Old Lace* (1921), *Sisters* (1922), *The Flame of the Yukon* (1926), and *The Rush Hour* (1927).

388

389

388. Alfred Paget (–). Alfred Paget gives superb performances as Belshazzar in *Intolerance* (1916) and as the gang leader in *The Musketeers of Pig Alley* (1912) under D. W. Griffith's direction. He disappeared from the screen in the 'teens and was dead by the twenties. Films include *Enoch Arden* (1915), *Nina, The Flower Girl* (1917), *Aladdin and the Wonderful Lamp* (1917), and *Cupid's Roundup* (1918).

389. Jean Paige (1896–). A Vitagraph actress from 1917 through 1924, Jean Paige married the company's co-founder, Albert E. Smith, in 1920. Films include *The Discounters of Money* (1917; her first film), *Tangled Lives* (1918), *Black Beauty* (1921), *The Prodigal Judge* (1922), and *Captain Blood* (1924; her last film).   **390. Eugene Pallette** (1889–1954). Eugene Pallette is best remembered as a portly, jovial character actor in talkies. Earlier, he was, if not dashing, at least a heavyweight leading man in silent films, playing the screen lover of Margery Wilson in the French story of *Intolerance* (1916). Films include *The Children in the House* (1916), *The Marcellini Millions* (1917), *Madam Who* (1918), *Fair and Warmer* (1919), *Alias Jimmy Valentine* (1920), *The Three Musketeers* (1921), *The Wolf Man* (1924), *Mantrap* (1926), and *Chicago* (1927).

390

392

391

391. Paul Panzer (1872–1958). Active through the forties, Panzer was one of the screen's first stars, beginning his career with Edison in 1905 and later moving to Vitagraph; he was the villain in the serial *The Perils of Pauline* (1914). Films include *Under Southern Skies* (1915), *Broken Fetters* (1916), *The Unchastened Woman* (1918), *When Knighthood Was in Flower* (1922), *The Fool* (1925), *The Johnstown Flood* (1926), and *Glorious Betsy* (1928).

392. Doris Pawn (1896–????). Doris Pawn was a Fox star of the 'teens who was first featured in comedies. *Motion Picture Classic* (October 1917) called her "a delicate bit of Western femininity." Films include *Blue Blood and Red* (1916), *The Spirit of '76* (1918), *What Happened to Rosa?* (1920), *Always the Woman* (1922), *The Hero* (1923), and *Fools and Riches* (1923; her last film).

394

393

393. Virginia Pearson (1888–1958). An actress who was good in vampire roles, Virginia Pearson could be quite exotic in her films when required. She was married to actor Sheldon Lewis. Films include *Aftermath* (1914), *The Turn of the Road* (1915), *Hypocrisy* (1916), *Royal Romance* (1917), *A Daughter of France* (1918), *The Bishop's Emeralds* (1919), *The Phantom of the Opera* (1925), *The Wizard of Oz* (1925), and *What Price Beauty* (1928).

394. Eileen Percy (1900–1973). A stage performer and magazine cover girl, Eileen Percy came to prominence in films as Douglas Fairbanks' leading lady in four 1917 features: *Wild and Woolly*, *Down to Earth*, *The Man From Painted Post*, and *Reaching for the Moon*. In the thirties, she wrote a gossip column for the Hearst newspapers. Films include *Where the West Begins* (1919), *Brass Buttons* (1919), *Told in the Hills* (1920), *Pardon My Nerve!* (1922), *Cobra* (1925), and *Backstage* (1927).

395

396

397

395. Jack Perrin (1896–1967). Jack Perrin began his career with Mack Sennett in 1917, but he came to fame after the First World War as a Western star. He was noted for his immaculate cowboy attire. Films include *Blind Husbands* (1919), *The Adorable Savage* (1920), *A Blue Jacket's Honor* (1922), *Lightnin' Jack* (1924), *The Man From Oklahoma* (1926), *Code of the Range* (1927), and *Plunging Hoofs* (1928). **396. Kathryn Perry** (1898–1983). A Ziegfeld *Follies* beauty, Kathryn Perry is best remembered for a series of Selznick comedies of the early twenties in which she starred with her husband, Owen Moore. Films include *Way Down East* (1920), *The Chicken in the Case* (1921), *Love Is An Awful Thing* (1922), *Main Street* (1923), *The First Year* (1926), and *Is Zat So?* (1927). **397. House Peters** (1880–1967). Publicized as "The Star of a Thousand Emotions," House Peters began his film career playing opposite Mary Pickford in *In the Bishop's Carriage* (1914). He retired after *Rose Marie* (1928), but he returned in 1952 for a guest appearance in *The Old West*. Films include *The Great Divide* (1915), *The Girl of the Golden West* (1918), *Lying Lips* (1921), *The Storm* (1922), and *Raffles, The Amateur Cracksman* (1925).

398

399

400

398. Olga Petrova (1884–1977). A major dramatic actress of the 'teens, Olga Petrova demanded feminist viewpoints in her films. Despite her name, she was born Muriel Harding in England, but always insisted on being addressed as Madame Petrova, except by her friends to whom she was simply Petrova. Films include *The Tigress* (1914; her first film), *The Heart of a Painted Woman* (1915), *The Undying Flame* (1917), and *The Panther Woman* (1918; her last film). Autobiography: *Butter with My Bread* (Indianapolis: Bobbs-Merrill, 1942). **399. Mary Philbin** (1903–). An actress who stood around and did nothing except look pretty in a considerable number of Universal features of the twenties. Films include *Merry-Go-Round* (1923), *The Phantom of the Opera* (1925), *Stella Maris* (1925), *The Man Who Laughs* (1927), *Surrender* (1927), and *Drums of Love* (1928). **400. Dorothy Phillips** (1892–1980). A fine dramatic star of Universal features in the late 'teens, Dorothy Phillips was married to director Allen Holubar. After her career as a star ended, she worked for more than thirty years as an extra. Films include *The Mark of Cain* (1916), *The Price of Silence* (1917), *A Doll's House* (1917), *Bondage* (1917), *The Heart of Humanity* (1919), *The Right to Happiness* (1919), *Man-Woman-Marriage* (1921), *The Sporting Chance* (1925), and *The Cradle Snatchers* (1927).

401

402

403

401. Jack Pickford (1896–1933). Mary Pickford's younger brother was noted for his boyish, almost impish, good looks. He began his career with D. W. Griffith at Biograph in 1909 and was active through the late twenties. Films include *Wildflower* (1914), *Seventeen* (1916), *Tom Sawyer* (1917), *The Little Shepherd of Kingdom Come* (1920), *The Good Woman* (1925), *Exit Smiling* (1926), and *Gang War* (1928; his last film).

402. Lottie Pickford (1895–1936). Younger sister of Mary, but never amounted to much and basically coasted on her sister's fame after beginning her career at American Biograph in 1909. Films include *The Two Paths* (1910), *The House of Bondage* (1914), *Fanchon the Cricket* (1915), *On the Level* (1917), *Mile-A-Minute Kendall* (1918), and *They Shall Pay* (1921).

403

403. Mary Pickford (1893–1979). Not the silent screen's greatest actress but certainly its biggest personality, Mary Pickford enjoyed a screen career that lasted from 1909 through 1933. Although better known today as a saccharine-sweet portrayer of children's roles, she was also a fine dramatic actress as witness her performances in *Stella Maris* (1918), *My Best Girl* (1927), and *Secrets* (1933; her last film). Films include *The Violin Maker of Cremona* (1909; her first film), *Tess of the Storm Country* (1914), *A Poor Little Rich Girl* (1917), *Rebecca of Sunnybrook Farm* (1917), *Pollyanna* (1920), *Rosita* (1923), *Sparrows* (1926), and *The Taming of the Shrew* (1929). Autobiography: *Sunshine and Shadow* (Garden City, NY: Doubleday, 1955). She appears in these photographs with her famous curls and as she looked after bobbing her hair.

404

405

404. ZaSu Pitts (1898–1963). Before the talkies established ZaSu Pitts as a comedienne, she was recognized as a major silent dramatic actress, thanks largely to her performance as Trina in *Greed* (1925). "She has the quality of infinite pity," commented Harry Carr in *The Los Angeles Times*. Films include *The Little Princess* (1917; her first film), *How Could You, Jean?* (1919), *The Goldfish* (1924), *Lazybones* (1925), and more than 100 sound productions concluding with *It's a Mad, Mad, Mad, Mad World* (1963).

405. Harry "Snub" Pollard (1889–1962). Sorrowful eyes and a droopy moustache were the trademarks of this actor who was on screen from 1915 through 1961. "Snub" Pollard was initially under contract to Hal Roach and played with Harold Lloyd. Films include *Captain Kidd's Kids* (1919), *Start Something* (1919), *The Stone Age* (1922), *It's A Gift* (1923), *The Courtship of Miles Sandwich* (1923), and *Once Over* (1928).

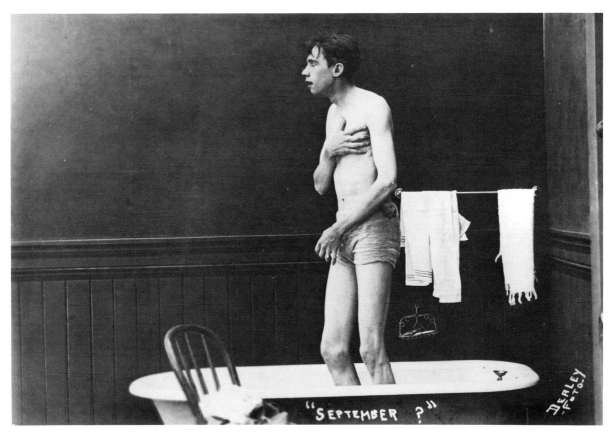

406

406. Victor Potel (1889–1947). A skinny comedian who began his career with Essanay in 1910 (where he remained through 1915), Victor Potel's roles were often minor but usually effective in a career which lasted through the forties. Films include *Quincy Adams Sawyer* (1922), *Anna Christie* (1923), *Women Who Give* (1924), and *What Price Beauty* (1928).

407

408

407. Arline Pretty (1893–1978). On screen from 1913 and ending her career as an extra, Arline Pretty was a Vitagraph leading lady of the mid- to late 'teens. Films include *The Thirteenth Girl* (1915), *The Secret Kingdom* (1917), *A Woman in Grey* (1920), *The Wages of Sin* (1921), *Rouged Lips* (1923), *The Primrose Path* (1925), and *Virgin Lips* (1928).   **408. Marie Prevost** (1895–1946). A Mack Sennett Bathing Beauty of the late 'teens, Marie Prevost developed into a competent, if lightweight actress of the twenties. Films include *Yankee Doodle in Berlin* (1919), *Brass* (1923), *The Marriage Circle* (1924), *Bobbed Hair* (1925), *Up in Mabel's Room* (1926), *Getting Gertie's Garter* (1927), and *The Godless Girl* (1929).   **409. Kate Price** (1872–1943). A plump and jovial comedienne, Kate Price played opposite Oliver Hardy in "Vim" comedies in 1917. She specialized in Irish landlady characterizations in the twenties. Films include *Jack Fat and Jim Slim at Coney Island* (1910; her first film), *Little Lord Fauntleroy* (1921), *The Spoilers* (1923), *The Sea Hawk* (1924), *His People* (1925), *The Cohens and the Kellys* (1926), *Orchids and Ermine* (1927), and *Show Girl* (1928).

409

AILEEN PRINGLE

410

411

412

410. Aileen Pringle (1895–). One of the more famous vamps of the twenties, thanks to her performance in Elinor Glyn's *Three Weeks* (1924), Aileen Pringle's career lasted from 1919 through 1943. She was under contract to Goldwyn/M-G-M from 1922 through 1929 and married to novelist James M. Cain (her second husband) from 1944 through 1947. Films include *The Christian* (1923), *A Thief in Paradise* (1925), *Soul Mates* (1925), *Body and Soul* (1927), *Puttin' on the Ritz* (1930), and *Jane Eyre* (1934).   **411. Edna Purviance** (1896–1958). Edna Purviance was Charlie Chapin's leading lady (from 1915–1923) whom he starred in *A Woman of Paris* (1923) and whose 1926 Josef von Sternberg-directed feature, *The Sea Gull*, he ordered destroyed. She was not a great actress, but she was adequate for the comedian's requirements. Films include *A Night Out* 1915; her first film), *Easy Street* (1917), *The Immigrant* (1917), *Shoulder Arms* (1918), *The Kid* (1921), and *The Pilgrim* (1923).   **412. Billy Quirk** (1873–1926). A light comedian who began at American Biograph in 1907 where he was known as "Muggsy." His career flourished when he joined Solax in 1911, but it declined in the late 'teens. Films include *What Happened to Father* (1915), *The Web of Life* (1917), *At the Stage Door* (1921), *My Old Kentucky Home* (1922), *Salomy Jane* (1923), and *The Dixie Handicap* (1925).

413

413. Esther Ralston (1902–). One of Paramount's top contract stars of the twenties, Esther Ralston displayed an elegance and quiet grace on screen beginning with her role as Mrs. Darling in *Peter Pan* (1924). She entered films as an extra in 1918, and her acting career continued through the sixties. Films include *Oliver Twist* (1922), *Beggar on Horseback* (1925), *A Kiss for Cinderella* (1926), *Old Ironsides* (1926), *The American Venus* (1926), and *The Case of Lena Smith* (1929). Autobiography: *Someday We'll Laugh* (Metuchen, NJ: Scarecrow Press, 1985).

414

415

414. Jobyna Ralston (1900–1967). Jobyna Ralston was likened by Adela Rogers St. Johns to "the refrain of a sweet, old-fashioned song." She was the perfect leading lady to Harold Lloyd in six films from 1923 through 1927, and had earlier been a leading lady to Max Linder in *The Three Must-Get-Theres* (1922). Films include *Girl Shy* (1924), *The Freshman* (1925), *For Heaven's Sake* (1926), *The Kid Brother* (1927), *Wings* (1927), and *The Toilers* (1928).

415. Natacha Rambova (1897–1966). Natacha Rambova was, in reality, Winifred Hudnot, daughter of the millionaire cosmetics manufacturer. She gained world renown when she married Rudolph Valentino in 1922 and celebrated the dissolution of the marriage with her one feature film appearance in *When Love Grows Cold* (1925). She was also a dilettante art director and costume designer, most notably for Nazimova.

416

417

418

416. Sally Rand (1904–1979). Sally Rand was a Cecil B. DeMille contract star of the mid- to late twenties who later gained fame for her fan dancing. Films include *The Road to Yesterday* (1925), *Braveheart* (1925), *Sunny Side Up* (1926), *The King of Kings* (1927), and *A Girl in Every Port* (1928). **417. Herbert Rawlinson** (1885–1953). A rugged leading man on screen from 1912 through 1951, Herbert Rawlinson was one of the busiest silent actors, at the height of his fame in the mid-'teens. Films include *The Sea Wolf* (1914), *Damon and Pythias* (1917), *The Turn of the Wheel* (1918), *The Common Cause* (1919), *The Scrapper* (1922), and *The Gilded Butterfly* (1926). **418. Charles Ray** (1891–1943). His roles as a bucolic young man making good became as tiresome for him as for his audiences, but when he tried to change with *The Courtship of Miles Standish* (1923), his days as a star ended. Films include *The Coward* (1915), *Peggy* (1916), *The Clodhopper* (1917), *Forty-Five Minutes From Broadway* (1920), *The Old Swimmin' Hole* (1921), and *The Garden of Eden* (1928).

419

419. Wallace Reid (1891–1923). A handsome leading man whose death from drug addiction gave the cinema one of its first major scandals. Wallace Reid entered films in 1910 and became a star with a 1915 Paramount contract. Films include *The Illumination* (1912), *The Birth of a Nation* (1915), *Enoch Arden* (1915), *Carmen* (1915), *The Woman God Forgot* (1917), *Excuse My Dust* (1920), *The Affairs of Anatol* (1921), and *Thirty Days* (1922; his last film).

420. Vera Reynolds (1899–1962). Vera Reynolds entered films with Christie Comedies in the early twenties and came to stardom with Cecil B. DeMille as a bright, bouncy heroine. Films include *The Golden Bed* (1925), *The Road to Yesterday* (1925), *Corporal Kate* (1926), and *Golf Widows* (1928). **421. Billie Rhodes** (1894–1988). A comedienne with all of the charm and less of the exuberance of Mabel Normand, Billie Rhodes began her career as an ingénue with the Kalem Company in 1913. Films include *The Big Horn Massacre* (1913), *Mrs. Plum's Pudding* (1915), *Putting Her Foot In It* (1916), *Black Hands and Soapsuds* (1917), *Hoop-La* (1919), *The Blue Bonnet* (1919), and *Leave It to Gerry* (1924; her last film). **422. Irene Rich** (1891–1988). Irene Rich was a statuesque, quietly commanding leading lady of stage, screen, and radio; she was often teamed opposite Will Rogers. Films include *The Girl in His House* (1918), *The Blue Bonnet* (1919), *Jes' Call Me Jim* (1920), *Boys Will Be Boys* (1921), *A Fool There Was* (1922), *Brass* (1923), *Beau Brummell* (1924), and *Lady Windermere's Fan* (1925).

420

421

422

423

423. Rin-Tin-Tin (1918–1932). Found by Lee Duncan in a French dugout during the First World War, Rin-Tin-Tin became the biggest moneymaker at Warner Bros. in the twenties. **Audrey Ferris** (1909–) entered films in 1926 and was the dog's leading lady in *Rinty of the Desert* (1928). Films include *The Lighthouse by the Sea* (1924), *Clash of the Wolves* (1925), *Tracked by the Police* (1927), and *A Race for a Life* (1928.) **424. Edith Roberts** (1899–1935). Edith Roberts was a Universal star who joined the company in 1914 as an extra, left it for a brief sojourn in Ziegfeld's *Midnight Frolic*, and later returned. She was good in comedies. Films include *Beans* (1918), *Lasca* (1919), *The Adorable Savage* (1920), *Pawned* (1922), *Seven Keys to Baldpate* (1925), and *The Jazz Girl* (1926).

424

425

425. Theodore Roberts (1861–1928). Theodore Roberts was ideal as an irate father or a harrassed, cigar-smoking businessman, usually in Cecil B. DeMille productions. His characterizations are perfectly summed up in *Roaring Road* (1919), in which a close-up of him changes to that of a bear. Films include *The Call of the North* (1914), *The Case of Becky* (1915), *Joan the Woman* (1916), *M'Liss* (1918), *Don't Change Your Wife* (1919), *Excuse My Dust* (1920), *The Affairs of Anatol* (1921), *Grumpy* (1923), *The Ten Commandments* (1923), and *The Cat's Pajamas* (1926).

426

427

426. Gertrude Robinson (1891–1962). An actress with the American Biograph company (1908–1913), Gertrude Robinson was active as a bit player or extra until 1957. In later years, Mary Pickford took care of her. Films include *Pippa Passes* (1909), *Lines of White On A Sullen Sea* (1909), *A Corner in Wheat* (1909), *Willful Peggy* (1910), and *Strongheart* (1913).

427. Earl Rodney (1888–1932). A light comedian usually in supporting roles at Keystone, which he joined in 1915, and elsewhere as the handsome juvenile. Films include *A Village Vampire* (1916), *Love Will Conquer* (1916), *An Oily Scoundrel* (1916), *The Biggest Show on Earth* (1918), *Chicken Hearted* (1921), and *Second Childhood* (1922).

428

429

428. Charles "Buddy" Rogers (1904–). An innocu
ous leading man in late silents and early talkies who
never again achieved the emotional intensity of his
performance in *Wings* (1927). A product of the
Paramount acting school, he always had to contend
with living in the shadow of his wife, Mary Pickford,
whose third and final husband he was. Films include
So's Your Old Man (1926), *My Best Girl* (1927), *Abie's
Irish Rose* (1928), *Follow Thru* (1930), and *Safety in
Numbers* (1930).

429. Will Rogers (1879–1935). Once America's
foremost entertainer and premiere philosopher, Will
Rogers made more than sixty features and shorts
between 1918 and 1935. Under contract to Goldwyn
from 1918 through 1921, he was a Hal Roach comedian
from 1923 through 1924, and a top box office star while
under contract to Fox from 1929 to his death. Films
include *Laughing Bill Hyde* (1918; his first film), *Jubilo*
(1919), *Doubling for Romeo* (1921), *The Headless Horseman* (1922), *Uncensored Movies* (1923), *Big Moments from
Little Pictures* (1924), and *A Texas Steer* (1927). Autobiography: *The Autobiography of Will Rogers* (Boston:
Houghton Mifflin, 1949).

430

430. Ruth Roland (1892–1937). She was the second greatest serial queen, every bit as attractive and athletic as her rival, Pearl White, and was in films from 1911 through 1935. Films include *Ruth Roland, The Kalem Girl* (1912), *Who Pays?* (1915 series), *Hands Up* (1918 serial), *The Adventures of Ruth* (1919 serial), and *Reno* (1930).

431

431. Ann Rork (1908–1988). One-time wife of oil magnate J. Paul Getty, Ann Rork had a brief stage career with the Pasadena Community Players before a career in supporting roles in the films produced by her father, Sam Rork, who died in 1933. Films include *Old Loves and New* (1927), *The Blond Saint* (1927), *The Notorious Lady* (1927), *The Prince of Headwaiters* (1927), and *A Texas Steer* (1927).

432

433

434

432. Alma Rubens (1897–1931). A gorgeous star of 'teens features whom one 1918 writer likened to "red roses in an onyx jar," Alma Rubens' career ended in tragedy when she died of drug addiction. She entered films with Vitagraph and gained prominence when she became Douglas Fairbanks' leading lady in 1916. At one time married to actor Ricardo Cortez. Films include *The Half-Breed* (1916), *The Americano* (1917), *The Crown of Destiny* (1917), *Under the Red Robe* (1923), *Cytherea* (1924), and *Show Boat* (1929). **433. William Russell** (1886–1929). A hefty, unromantic hero, perfectly cast as Matt in *Anna Christie* (1923), William Russell entered films in 1911 and remained active until his death. Films include *The Straight Road* (1914), *The Diamond from the Sky* (1915 serial), *Sealed Lips* (1915), *Boston Blackie* (1923), *The Beloved Brute* (1924), *The Girl From Chicago* (1927), and *Girls Gone Wild* (1929; his last film). **434. Al St. John** (1892–1963). Al St. John was a skinny comedian who specialized in "rube" roles from Keystone in the early 'teens through Educational in the twenties. Later, he was a supporting actor in Westerns. Films include *Tillie's Punctured Romance* (1914), *Fatty and Mabel Adrift* (1916), *The Butcher Boy* (1917), *The Happy Pest* (1921), *The Hayseed* (1921), *The Garden of Weeds* (1924), and *American Beauty* (1927).

435

436

435. Marin Sais (1890–1971). Primarily associated with the Kalem Company where she was a leading lady from 1911 through 1917, Marin Sais was on screen from 1909 through 1950. Films include *Shannon of the Sixth* (1914), *The Pitfall* (1915), *The Vanity Pool* (1918), *Bonds of Honor* (1919), *Riders of the Law* (1922), *The Measure of a Man* (1924), and *The Wild Horse Stampede* (1926.)   **436. Monroe Salisbury** (1876–1935). Monroe Salisbury was a Universal leading man of the 'teens. Co-star Ruth Clifford, who acted opposite him in love scenes, recalled her shock at discovering just how old he was in their love scenes and that he wore a wig. Films include *Brewster's Millions* (1914), *The Lamb* (1915), *Ramona* (1916), *The Savage* (1917), *The Light of Victory* (1919), *The Barbarian* (1920), and *The Great Alone* (1922).

437

439

438

437. Teddy Sampson (1898–1970). From vaudeville with Gus Edwards, Teddy Sampson graduated to films with D. W. Griffith. She married comedian Ford Sterling, which, perhaps, accounts for her early twenties career in Supreme Comedies for Al Christie. Films include *Home, Sweet Home* (1914), *The Fox Woman* (1915), *Cross Currents* (1916), *Her American Husband* (1918), *Fighting for Gold* (1919), *Bits of Life* (1921), *Outcast* (1922), and *The Bad Man* (1923). **438. Thomas Santschi** (1880–1931). He was a Selig leading man of the early 'teens who lost the climactic fight in *The Spoilers* (1914) to William Farnum, leading to those immortal words: "I broke him with my hands." Films include *The Adventures of Kathlyn* (1913), *The Garden of Allah* (1916), *Little Orphant Annie* (1918), *Shadows* (1919), *The Cradle of Courage* (1920), *The Plunderer* (1924), *Paths to Paradise* (1925), *The Third Degree* (1926), and *Tracked by the Police* (1927). **439. Jackie Saunders** (1897–1954). After entering films with American Biograph in 1911, Jackie Saunders became a star at the Balboa Company in the mid-'teens. Films include *The Will o' the Wisp* (1914), *Rose of the Alley* (1916), *Drag Harlan* (1920), *Puppets of Fate* (1921), *Shattered Reputations* (1923), *Alimony* (1924), and *The People vs. Nancy Preston* (1925).

441

442

440. Joseph Schildkraut (1895–1964). A stage actor on Broadway and in his native Vienna, Joseph Schildkraut will always be associated with the roles of Judas Iscariot in *The King of Kings* (1927), Gaylord Ravenal in *Show Boat* (1929), and Otto Frank in *The Diary of Anne Frank* (1959). Films include *Orphans of the Storm* (1921; his first U. S. film), *The Road to Yesterday* (1925), *Young April* (1926), and *The Heart Thief* (1927). Autobiography: *My Father and I* (New York: Viking, 1959).   **441. Larry Semon** (1889–1928). A slapstick comedian who began his film career at Vitagraph as a director in 1916, Larry Semon began acting before the cameras a year later. He left Vitagraph in 1923, and as his ego grew larger, his career grew smaller. Films include *Boasts and Boldness* (1917; his first film as an actor), *Frauds and Frenzies* (1918), *School Days* (1920), *The Sawmill* (1921), *The Girl in the Limousine* (1924), *The Wizard of Oz* (1925), and *Underworld* (1927; his last film).

442. Mack Sennett (1880–1960). The man most closely associated with the production of slapstick comedy, Mack Sennett began his career as an actor at American Biograph (1908 through 1912) before the formation of his Keystone Company. Films include *The Curtain Pole* (1908), *The Gibson Goddess* (1909), *Cured* (1911), *The Diving Girl* (1911), and *What The Doctor Ordered* (1912). Autobiography: *King of Comedy* (Garden City, NY: Doubleday, 1954).

443

444

443. Clarine Seymour (1900–1920). A tragic, early death ended a career that might have made Clarine Seymour a light comedienne even better than Dorothy Gish. On screen from 1917, she was D. W. Griffith's last major discovery. Films include *The Mystery of the Double Cross* (1917 serial), *The Girl Who Stayed at Home* (1919), *True Heart Susie* (1919), *Scarlet Days* (1919), and *The Idol Dancer* (1920; her last film).

444. Norma Shearer (1900–1983). In films such as *The Student Prince in Old Heidelberg* (1927), Norma Shearer displays a wistful tenderness that she lost with the coming of sound. On screen from 1920 through 1942, she was closely associated with M-G-M (under contract from 1923) and married to producer Irving Thalberg from 1927 until his death in 1936. Films include *He Who Gets Slapped* (1924), *The Tower of Lies* (1925), *The Devil's Circus* (1926), *The Demi-Bride* (1927), *After Midnight* (1927), *The Actress* (1928), and more than twenty sound features.

445

447

446

445. Lowell Sherman (1888–1934). Lowell Sherman is best known as the suave and villainous Lennox Sanderson, who seduces Lillian Gish in *Way Down East* (1920), his screen debut. The sophistication of his roles in silent films is matched by many of the films he directed in the thirties. Films include *Molly O'* (1921), *Grand Larceny* (1922), *Monsieur Beaucaire* (1924), *The Reckless Lady* (1926), and *The Garden of Eden* (1928). **446. Nell Shipman** (1892–1970). A Canadian-born actress and director who specialized in outdoor subjects, Nell Shipman made her debut in 1915. Her extant films hardly seem to justify the importance that some historians attach to her work. Films include *God's Country and the Woman* (1916), *The Black Wolf* (1917), *Back to God's Country* (1919), *Something New* (1920), and *The Girl From God's Country* (1921). Autobiography: *The Silent Screen & My Talking Heart* (Boise, ID: Boise State University, 1987). **447. Gertrude Short** (1902–1968). Short by name and short in stature, this actress was great in sidekick roles. She began her stage career at the age of five years and entered films with Edison a few years later. Films include *The Little Angel of Canyon Creek* (1914), *The Little Princess* (1917), *Riddle Gawne* (1918), *Boy Crazy* (1922), *The Gold Diggers* (1923), *Barbara Frietchie* (1924), *Beggar on Horseback* (1925), *Ladies of Leisure* (1926), and *Tillie the Toiler* (1927).

448

449

448. George Siegmann (1882–1928). A superb villain who destroyed Babylon in *Intolerance* (1916) and terrorized Lillian Gish in *Hearts of the World* (1918). Films include *The Avenging Conscience* (1914), *The Birth of a Nation* (1915), *The Little Yank* (1917), *A Connecticut Yankee in King Arthur's Court* (1920), *The Queen of Sheba* (1921), *Oliver Twist* (1922), *Anna Christie* (1923), and *The Cat and the Canary* (1927). **Milton Sills**, see entry No. 273.   **449. Phillips Smalley** (1865–1939). Phillips Smalley was a portly, slightly stuffy actor who co-directed with his wife, Lois Weber (married 1904–1922) and appeared as a supporting performer in many films through the thirties. Films include *False Colors* (1914), *Idle Wives* (1916), *Saving the Family Name* (1916), *The Hand That Rocks the Cradle* (1917), *Too Wise Wives* (1921), *Cameo Kirby* (1923), *Charley's Aunt* (1925), and *Sensation Seekers* (1927).   **450. Marguerite Snow** (1889–1958). An important Thanhouser leading lady from 1911 through 1915, Marguerite Snow was married to director James Cruze (divorced in 1922). She was George M. Cohan's leading lady in his first film, *Broadway Jones* (1917), but her career did not last beyond the 'teens. Films include *Baseball and Bloomers* (1911; her first film), *She* (1912), *The Million Dollar Mystery* (1914), *Zudora* (1915), *The Faded Flower* (1916), and *In His Brother's Place* (1919).

450

451

452

453

451. Pauline Starke (1901–1977). A simple and innocent-looking ingénue of the 'teens discovered by D. W. Griffith, Pauline Starke graduated to playing glamorized roles in the twenties. Films include *The Birth of a Nation* (1915), *Intolerance* (1916), *The Wharf Rat* (1916), *Until They Get Me* (1917), *A Connecticut Yankee in King Arthur's Court* (1921), *Little Church Around the Corner* (1923), and *The Viking* (1929).   **452. Myrtle Stedman** (1885–1938). Myrtle Stedman entered films in 1912 with Selig working under the direction of her husband, Marshall Stedman (separated in 1920). She was active as a featured player in the twenties and as a character actress in the thirties until her death. Films include *The Valley of the Moon* (1914), *Jane* (1915), *The Call of the Cumberlands* (1916), *Sex* (1920), *Reckless Youth* (1922), *Bread* (1924), *Don Juan's Three Nights* (1926), and *Alias the Deacon* (1928).   **453. Ford Sterling** (1884–1939). A Mack Sennett comedian from 1911 through 1921 and the police chief of Sennett's Keystone Kops, Ford Sterling developed into a reliable character comedian in the twenties. He was married to Teddy Sampson. Films include *Yankee Doodle in Berlin* (1918), *Love, Honor and Behave* (1920), *So Big* (1924), *The American Venus* (1926), and *Casey at the Bat* (1927).

454. Anita Stewart (1895–1961). Anita Stewart joined Vitagraph in 1911 and became one of the company's major stars, usually partnered with Earle Williams. Films include *A Million Bid* (1914), *The Juggernaut* (1915), *The Goddess* (1915 serial), *Virtuous Wives* (1919), *In Old Kentucky* (1919), and *Never the Twain Shall Meet* (1925).   **455. Roy Stewart** (1883–1933). A Western star of the 'teens, Roy Stewart proved himself to be capable of dramatic roles in the twenties, which answered a critic who demanded, "Where would Roy Stewart be without a horse to lean on?" Films include *The House Built Upon Sand* (1916), *Untamed* (1918), *Riders of the Dawn* (1920), *The Love Brand* (1923), *Time, The Comedian* (1925), *Sparrows* (1926), and *The Viking* (1929).   **456. Lewis Stone** (1878–1953). Before he became Judge Hardy in the Andy Hardy series at M-G-M, Lewis Stone had been a somewhat mature-looking leading man in silent films from 1916. He alternated between the stage and screen in the 'teens, and got his big break in Rex Ingram's *The Prisoner of Zenda* (1922). Films include *Honor's Altar* (1916; his first film), *The River's End* (1920), *Trifling Women* (1922), *Scaramouche* (1923), *The Lost World* (1925), *Don Juan's Three Nights* (1926), *The Private Life of Helen of Troy* (1927), and a hundred other features over the next three decades.

455

454

456

457

458

457. Ruth Stonehouse (1892–1941). A dancer on stage, Ruth Stonehouse became a featured star at Universal in 1916 after three years with Essanay. Films include *The Slim Princess* (1915), *Love Never Dies* (1916), *Love Aflame* (1917), *The Land of Jazz* (1920), *Flames of Passion* (1923), *Blood and Steel* (1925), and *The Satin Woman* (1927).

458. Edith Storey (1892–1955). One of the more distinctive of Vitagraph actresses, Edith Storey was with the company from 1909 through 1917 (except for a brief sojourn with Gaston Méliès in Texas). She is seen at her best in *A Florida Enchantment* (1914). Films include *A Tale of Two Cities* (1911), *The Troublesome Stepdaughters* (1912), *The Island of Regeneration* (1915), *The Silent Woman* (1919), and *The Greater Profit* (1921; her last film).

459. Erich von Stroheim (1885–1957). A super-egotist, but also one of the very few creative geniuses to come out of the American cinema. On screen as a actor from the mid-'teens, von Stroheim became a director with *Blind Husbands* (1919); during the twenties, he left his acting career in abeyance while directing *Greed* (1925) and *The Merry Widow* (1925). Films include *Old Heidelberg* (1915), *The Social Secretary* (1916), *Hearts of the World* (1918), *The Heart of Humanity* (1919), *Foolish Wives* (1922), and *The Great Gabbo* (1929).

460. Strongheart (1916–1929). An important dog star of the twenties, Strongheart was trained by Larry Trimble and paved the way for Rin-Tin-Tin. He was so popular that he was even the subject of a book, *Letters to Strongheart*, edited by J. Allen Boone (New York: Prentice-Hall, 1940). Films include *The Silent Call* (1921), *Brawn of the North* (1922), *The Love Master* (1924), *White Fang* (1925), and *The Return of Boston Blackie* (1927).

459

460

461

462

461. Gloria Swanson (1899–1983). Gloria Swanson entered films with Essanay in 1915 and became a star under Cecil B. DeMille's tutelage in 1919. She became one of the screen's more glamorous stars with Paramount in the twenties, and with *Sunset Boulevard* (1950), she became a living legend. Films include *Male and Female* (1919), *The Affairs of Anatol* (1921), *Beyond the Rocks* (1922), *Zaza* (1923), *Manhandled* (1924), *Madame Sans-Gêne* (1925), and *Sadie Thompson* (1928). Autobiography: *Swanson on Swanson* (New York: Random House, 1980).

462. Blanche Sweet (1896–1986). An engagingly outspoken silent star, Blanche Sweet commenced her film career in 1909 after a stage career that began in the last century. She was, with Mary Pickford, D. W. Griffith's first major dramatic star. When she left Griffith in 1914, she starred for Cecil B. DeMille and for her first husband, Marshall Neilan, and reached the zenith of her career with a performance in the title role of *Anne Christie* (1923). Films include *The Lonedale Operator* (1911), *The Painted Lady* (1912), *Judith of Bethulia* (1913), *Home, Sweet Home* (1914), *The Avenging Conscience* (1914), *The Warrens of Virginia* (1915), *The Unpardonable Sin* (1919), *Quincy Adams Sawyer* (1922), *Tess of the D'Urbervilles* (1924), *The Sporting Venus* (1925), and *Showgirl in Hollywood* (1930).

463. Josef Swickard (1866–1940). Born in Germany and Germanic in appearance, Josef Swickard was on screen from 1912 through 1928. He was an impressive character actor best remembered for his performance as Marcelo Desnoyers in *The Four Horsemen of the Apocalypse* (1921). Films include *A Tale of Two Cities* (1917), *The Light of Western Skies* (1918), *Blind Youth* (1920), *The Golden Gift* (1922), *Easy Money* (1925), *Officer Jim* (1926), and *False Morals* (1927).   **464. Mabel Taliaferro** (1887–1979). She was a stage actress featured in a number of films from 1911 through 1921 when she returned to the theatre to renew a career that lasted another four decades. Films include *The Three Of Us* (1914), *The Dawn of Love* (1916), *A Wife By Proxy* (1917), *The Rich Slave* (1920), and *Sentimental Tommy* (1921).   **465. Constance Talmadge** (1899–1973). Despite a brilliant comedic performance as the Mountain Girl in *Intolerance* (1916), Constance Talmadge never achieved the success of her sister Norma. She made her debut in 1914 with Vitagraph, had her own production company in the late 'teens, and retired from the screen in 1929. Films include *The Matrimaniac* (1916), *A Pair of Silk Stockings* (1918), *A Virtuous Vamp* (1919), *Dulcy* (1923), *The Goldfish* (1924), and *Venus* (1929; her last film).

464

463

465

466

467

466. Natalie Talmadge (1899–1969). The least active in films of the Talmadge sisters, she made a handful of films in the 'teens and only two features in the twenties: *The Passion Flower* (1921) and *Our Hospitality* (1923). She supported her husband, Buster Keaton (married in 1921; divorced in 1933), in the latter film.

467. Norma Talmadge (1897–1957). One of the finest silent screen dramatic stars, Norma Talmadge had an expressive face particularly suited to tragedy. She entered films in 1910 at Vitagraph and attracted attention with a "bit" part in *A Tale of Two Cities* (1911). Her first husband, Joseph Schenck (married 1916–1934), created the Norma Talmadge Film Company in 1916. Her second husband was George Jessel (married 1934–1937). Films include *The Battle Cry of Peace* (1915), *Panthea* (1917), *Smilin' Through* (1922), *The Eternal Flame* (1922), *Secrets* (1924), *Kiki* (1926), *Camille* (1927), and *DuBarry: Woman of Passion* (1930; her last film).

468

469

468. Richard Talmadge (1896–1981). Richard Talmadge was a leading man of "B" action pictures who earlier performed stunts for Douglas Fairbanks in *The Mollycoddle* (1920), *The Mark of Zorro* (1920), *The Nut* (1921), and *The Three Musketeers* (1921). Films include *The Unknown* (1921), *Taking Chances* (1922), *Speed King* (1923), *The Prince of Pep* (1925), and *Doubling with Danger* (1926).

469. Rose Tapley (1881–1956). On screen through the thirties, Rose Tapley made her debut in 1905 and was active in the late 'teens promoting "better pictures." Films include *Vanity Fair* (1911), *The Illumination* (1912), *Java Head* (1923), *The Pony Express* (1925), and *It* (1927).

470

470. Estelle Taylor (1894–1958). An underrated dramatic actress, she began her film career doubling for Dorothy Dalton while appearing on stage at night. Estelle Taylor was superb in films as varied as *While New York Sleeps* (1920) and *Street Scene* (1931); married to Jack Dempsey. Films include *The Golden Shower* (1919), *Monte Cristo* (1922), *The Ten Commandments* (1923), *The Alaskan* (1924), and *Don Juan* (1926).

471

472

471. Conway Tearle (1878–1938). A handsome. slightly older leading man, Conway Tearle was ideally suited to play opposite young beauties such as Norma Talmadge or Corinne Griffith. He entered films in the early 'teens and remained active until his death. Films include *The Common Law* (1916), *The Foolish Virgin* (1916), *The Fall of the Romanoffs* (1917), *Stella Maris* (1918), *A Virtuous Vamp* (1919), *The Eternal Flame* (1922), *Bella Donna* (1923), *Black Oxen* (1924), and *Dancing Mothers* (1926).

472. Lou Tellegen (1883–1934). A tragic actor, and former stage and French film leading man to actress Sarah Bernhardt, Lou Tellegen was adequate as Geraldine Farrar's leading man on screen. The title of his autobiography explains his success. Films include *The Explorer* (1915; his first U. S. film), *The World and Its Woman* (1919), *The Woman and the Puppet* (1920), *Between Friends* (1924), *The Redeeming Sin* (1925), *East Lynne* (1925), and *Enemies of the Law* (1931; his last film). Autobiography: *Women Have Been Kind* (New York: Vanguard Press, 1931).

473

474

473. Alice Terry (1901–1987). An unpretentious actress who, wearing a blonde wig, usually starred in the films of her husband, Rex Ingram (married in 1921 until his death in 1950). She began her career as an extra with Crystal and Thomas H. Ince in the early 'teens, and was a Metro/M-G-M contract star from 1920 through 1927. Very beautiful and probably a better actress than her roles might suggest. Films include *The Four Horsemen of the Apocalypse* (1921), *The Conquering Power* (1921), *The Prisoner of Zenda* (1922), *Scaramouche* (1923), *Confessions of a Queen* (1925), *Mare Nostrum* (1926), and *The Garden of Allah* (1927).

474. Olive Thomas (1898–1920). Olive Thomas was a Selznick screen star who was a beautiful showgirl in the Ziegfeld *Follies* and other Broadway revues. She died of a drug overdose shortly after her marriage to Jack Pickford. Films include *Broadway Arizona* (1917), *Betty Takes a Hand* (1918), *The Follies Girl* (1919), *Love's Prisoner* (1919), and *The Flapper* (1920).

475

476

475. Fred Thomson (1890–1928). Fred Thomson deserted a career as a minister to begin a screen career as Mary Pickford's leading man. He married screen-writer Frances Marion in 1919 and later became a cowboy star in the style of Tom Mix. Films include *The Love Light* (1921; his first film), *Just Around the Corner* (1921), *Penrod* (1922), *A Chapter in Her Life* (1923), *Thundering Hoofs* (1924), *Lone Hand Saunders* (1926), and *Arizona Nights* (1927).

476. Fay Tincher (–). A D. W. Griffith discovery, Fay Tincher made her screen debut in *The Battle of the Sexes* (1914). Best known for the comedy series: "Ethel and Bill" (1914–1915) and "The Gumps" (1925). Films include *Home, Sweet Home* (1914), *Don Quixote* (1916), and *Excitement* (1924).

477

478

477. Ernest Torrence (1878–1933). One of the
great villains of the screen as exemplified by his performances as Luke Hatburn in *Tol'able David* (1921) and
Captain Hook in *Peter Pan* (1924). His characters
always seemed more associated with the country than
the city. Films include *The Hunchback of Notre Dame*
(1923), *The Covered Wagon* (1923), *The Pony Express*
(1923), *Mantrap* (1926), and *Steamboat Bill, Jr.*
(1928).   **478. Raquel Torres** (1908–1987). Raquel
Torres made only two silent features — *White Shadows in
the South Seas* (1928) and *The Desert Rider* (1929) — but
the former is a classic, thanks in part to her natural
acting ability, which never reappeared in later sound
films such as *Under a Texas Moon* (1930) and *Duck Soup*
(1933).

479

479. Glenn Tryon (1899–1970). Active from the mid-twenties, Glenn Tryon was a competent actor with a raw and tough underlying quality. He was at his best in *Lonesome* (1928). Later, was a writer, producer, and director. Films include *The Battling Orioles* (1924), *The Poor Nut* (1927), *Hot Heels* (1928), and *The Gate Crasher* (1928).   **480. Mabel Trunnelle** (1879–1981). An Edison star from 1910 through 1917 with a short break at Majestic in 1911, Mabel Trunnelle often co-starred with her husband, Herbert Prior. Films include *A Modern Cinderella* (1911), *The Man He Might Have Been* (1913), *Eugene Aram* (1915), *Ransom's Folly* (1915), *The Heart of the Hills* (1916), and *The Ghost of Old Morro* (1917).

480

481

482

481. Florence Turner (1887–1946). The first star of the Vitagraph Company, which she joined in 1907, Florence Turner was also, arguably, the screen's first star. She was a talented actress who also starred in British films between 1913 and 1916, and 1922 and 1924. In the twenties, she became a "bit" player; a decade later, she became an extra. Films include *A Dixie Mother* (1910), *A Tale of Two Cities* (1911), *Jealousy* (1911), *A Vitagraph Romance* (1912), *Fool's Gold* (1919), and *College* (1927).   **482. Ben Turpin** (1869–1940). This cross-eyed comedian whose antics were described by critic James Agee as "like Paderewski assaulting a climax" was on screen from 1907 until 1940. He was with Essanay for the first nine years of his career and later was associated with Mack Sennett. He presents a brilliant parody of Erich von Stroheim in *Three Foolish Weeks* (1924). Films include *Ben Gets a Duck and Is Ducked* (1907; his first film), *His New Job* (1915), *Are Waitresses Safe?* (1917), *Uncle Tom Without a Cabin* (1919), *A Small Town Idol* (1921), *The Shriek of Araby* (1923), *Yukon Jake* (1924), and *Hogan's Alley* (1925).

483

484

483. Lenore Ulrich (1892–1970). A David Belasco
stage star, Lenore Ulrich filmed her great theatrical
success of 1917, *Tiger Rose*, in 1923. She made a few
features in the late 'teens and enjoyed a later film career
in early talkies from 1929. Films include *The Better
Woman* (1915), *Her Own People* (1917), and *Roses and
Thorns* (1919).   **484. Rudolph Valentino** (1895–
1926). The best known of all male silent stars,
Rudolph Valentino exuded a sensuality that is still
apparent in his films, despite his obvious lack of acting
ability. He began as an extra in the mid-'teens and
came to stardom with *The Four Horsemen of the Apocalypse*
(1921); his best acting effort was in the lesser-known
Moran of the Lady Letty (1922). Films include *A Society
Sensation* (1918), *Eyes of Youth* (1919), *The Wonderful
Chance* (1920), *The Sheik* (1921), *Camille* (1921), *Blood
and Sand* (1922), *Monsieur Beaucaire* (1924), *The Eagle*
(1925), and *The Son of the Sheik* (1926; his last film).

485

485. **Virginia Valli** (1895–1968). A Universal
contract star of the twenties who came to fame with *The
Storm* (1922), Virginia Valli was the star of Alfred
Hitchcock's first feature, *The Pleasure Garden* (1925).
She retired from the screen in the early thirties after
her marriage to actor Charles Farrell. Films include *His
Father's Wife* (1919), *The Black Circle* (1919), *Sentimental
Tommy* (1921), *The Shock* (1923), *K-The Unknown*
(1924), *Up the Ladder* (1925), and *Marriage* (1927). **486.
Wally Van** (1880–1974). A Vitagraph comedian from
1910 through 1916 who starred in the "Cutey" series of
light comedies and later became a minor director and
producer. Films include *Cutey and the Chorus Girls*
(1913), *The Fortune* (1913), *Bunny's Dilemma* (1913),
Cutey's Vacation (1914), *Doctor Polly* (1914), *The Chief's
Goat* (1915), *Cutey's Sister* (1915), and *When Hooligan
and Dooligan Ran for Mayor* (1916).

486

487

488

487. Victor Varconi (1891–1976). Hungarian-born actor who began his screen career in his native land in 1913 and was often associated with Alexander Korda. Victor Varconi came to the U. S. in 1924 and was on screen through 1959. Films include *Feet of Clay* (1924), *The Volga Boatman* (1926), *The King of Kings* (1927), *The Forbidden Woman* (1927), and *Chicago* (1927). Autobiography: *It's Not Enough to be Hungarian* (Santa Barbara, CA: Graphic Impressions, 1976).   **488. Bobby Vernon** (1897–1939). A comic juvenile best known for *Teddy at the Throttle* (1917), in which he rescues Gloria Swanson, Bobby Vernon was on screen from 1913 (with Universal Joker Comedies) until his death. Films include *Love and Electricity* (1914), *Fickle Fatty's Fall* (1915), *The Sultan's Wife* (1917), *Second Childhood* (1922), *French Pastry* (1925), and *Footloose Widows* (1926).   **489. Florence Vidor** (1895–1977). An actress of quiet dignity and radiant beauty, in films from 1916, Florence Vidor took her name from director King Vidor, whom she married in 1915. Films include *A Tale of Two Cities* (1917), *Old Wives for New* (1918), *The Jack-Knife Man* (1920), *Hail the Woman* (1922), *Alice Adams* (1923), *Are Parents People?* (1925), *Eagle of the Sea* (1927), and *Chinatown Nights* (1929; her last film).

489

490

490. Marie Walcamp (1894–1936). A pretty little blonde actress, Marie Walcamp began her screen career at Universal and never really got the breaks she deserved. She died a suicide. Films include *The Evil* *Power* (1913), *Liberty, A Daughter of the U. S. A.* (1916), *Patria* (1917), *The Blot* (1921), *A Desperate Adventure* (1924), and *In a Moment of Temptation* (1927).

491

492

491. Ethel Wales (1878–1952). A little-known, but very good actress at Paramount in the early to mid-twenties, Ethel Wales specialized in playing older women. She was memorable in *Miss Lulu Bett* (1921). Films include *Bobbed Hair* (1922), *The Covered Wagon* (1923), *Merton of the Movies* (1924), *Beggar on Horseback* (1925), and *The Girl in the Pullman* (1927).

492. Lillian Walker (1887–1975). A Vitagraph leading lady (1911–1917) who was famous for her dimple, Lillian Walker was active on screen through 1922. Films include *The Inherited Taint* (1911; her first film), *The Troublesome Stepdaughters* (1912), *Green Stockings* (1916), *The Star Gazer* (1917), *The Woman God Changed* (1921), and *Love's Boomerang* (1922).

493. George Walsh (1889–1981). Brother of director Raoul Walsh and a major Fox star from 1916 through 1921, George Walsh was signed for the title role in *Ben-Hur*, (1926) was replaced by Ramon Novarro and ended his career in "B" features. Films include *Intolerance* (1916), *The Honor System* (1917), *On The Jump* (1918), *Vanity Fair* (1923), *Reno* (1923), and *The Prince of Broadway* (1926).

GEORGE WALSH

494

495

494. Henry B. Walthall (1878–1936). Walthall gives his greatest performance as the Little Colonel in *The Birth of a Nation* (1915) and never really displayed that same emotional acting ability again until talkies such as *Judge Priest* (1934). After a lengthy stage career, he entered films with D. W. Griffith in 1909 and might have prospered more had he stayed with that director. Films include *A Convict's Sacrifice* (1909; his first film), *Judith of Bethulia* (1913), *Home, Sweet Home* (1914), *The Avenging Conscience* (1914), *The Scarlet Letter* (1927), *Abraham Lincoln* (1930), and *The Devil Doll* (1936).

495. H. B. Warner (1875–1958). On stage from 1883 and on screen from 1914, H. B. Warner will always be associated with two roles: Christ in *The King of Kings* (1927) and Chang in *Lost Horizon* (1937). Films include *The Lost Paradise* (1914; his first film), *The Beggar of Cawnpore* (1916), *God's Man* (1917), *Zaza* (1923), and *Liliom* (1930).

496

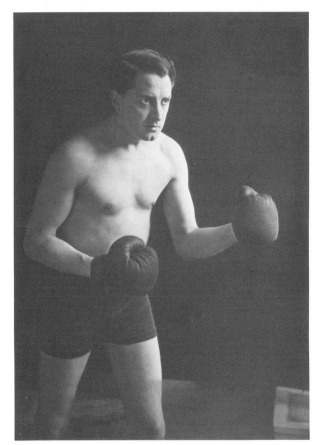

497

496. Robert Warwick (1878–1964). A star with the World Film Company and Famous Players in the 'teens, Robert Warwick always appeared reliable and domestic; he enjoyed a lengthy sound career. Films include *The Dollar Mark* (1914; his first film), *Alias Jimmy Valentine* (1915), *Friday the Thirteenth* (1916), *The Argyle Case* (1917), *In Mizzoura* (1919), *Jack Straw* (1920), and *The Spitfire* (1924). **497. Bryant Washburn** (1884–1963). Best remembered for the "Skinner" comedies, Bryant Washburn began his screen career in 1911 with Essanay, where he remained for seven years. He specialized in light comedy and became a character player with the coming of sound. Films include *Skinner's Dress Suit* (1917), *It Pays to Advertise* (1919), *Mrs. Temple's Telegram* (1920), *Too Much Johnson* (1920), *Rupert of Hentzau* (1923), and *The Wizard of Oz* (1925).

499

498

498. Niles Welch (1888–1976). After a screen debut with Vitagraph, Welch became a Metro leading man who co-starred in the first Technicolor feature: *The Gulf Between* (1918). Films include *A Royal Family* (1915), *Merely Mary Ann* (1916), *The Virtuous Thief* (1919), *The Spenders* (1920), *Reckless Youth* (1922), *Wine of Youth* (1924), and *Faithful Wives* (1926).   **499. Winifred Westover** (1900–1978). William S. Hart's leading lady and, later, his wife (married in 1921; separated a year later), Winifred Westover retired from the screen with the birth of her son in 1922, but she made a triumphant return in the title role of *Lummox* (1930). Films include *The Matrimaniac* (1916), *Jim Bludso* (1917), *John Petticoats* (1919), *The Village Sleuth* (1920), *If Life Worth Living?* (1921), and *Love's Masquerade* (1922).

500

500. Alice White (1907–1983). Alice White was an actress who made an art of vulgarity. She became a star as Dorothy Shaw, the friend of Lorelei Lee, in *Gentlemen Prefer Blondes* (1928) and was hopelessly common as the original "show girl" in silents and early talkies. Films include *American Beauty* (1927), *The Private Life of Helen of Troy* (1927), *Harold Teen* (1928), *Lingerie* (1928), and *Show Girl* (1928).

502

503

501. Pearl White (1889–1938). The best
known — in fact, legendary — silent serial queen, Pearl
White had a beauty and charm (albeit melodramatic)
that should have, but did not, assure her stardom in
straight features. She appeared on screen from 1910
through 1925. Films include *The Perils of Pauline* (1914
serial), *The Exploits of Elaine* (1915 serial), *The Iron Claw*
(1916 serial), *The White Moll* (1920), *Plunder* (1922
serial), and *Terror* (1925). Autobiography: *Just Me*
(New York: George H. Doran, 1919). **502. Crane
Wilbur** (1886–1973). "A regular fellow" is how *The
Moving Picture World* (November 14, 1914) described
Crane Wilbur, who was Pearl White's leading man in
The Perils of Pauline (1914). Later, he became a writer,
responsible for, among other films, *The House of Wax*
(1953). Films include *The Corsair* (1914), *Vengeance Is
Mine* (1916), *The Single Code* (1917), *Stripped for a
Million* (1919), *Something Different* (1920), and *The
Heart of Maryland* (1921).

503. Clara Williams (1888–1928). Ince contract star
of the 'teens with very distinctive features. Films
include *The Bargain* (1914), *The Italian* (1915), *Hell's
Hinges* (1916), *The Market of Vain Desire* (1916), *Paws of
the Bear* (1917), and *Carmen of the Klondike* (1918).

504

504. Earle Williams (1880–1927). A popular leading man usually partnered with Anita Stewart, Earle Williams began his screen career with Vitagraph in 1911 and remained with that company until 1923.

Films include *The Christian* (1914), *The Juggernaut* (1915), *The Goddess* (1915 serial), *Arsene Lupin* (1917), *Restless Souls* (1922), *Masters of Men* (1923), *Lena Rivers* (1925), and *Diplomacy* (1926).

505

505. Kathlyn Williams (1888–1960). The star of the screen's first serial, *The Adventures of Kathlyn* (1913–1914), Kathlyn Williams was also a capable dramatic actress as evidenced by her mature performance in *Conrad in Quest of His Youth* (1920). She entered films in 1909 with American Biograph, was a Selig contract star from 1910 through 1917, and under contract to Paramount from 1917 through 1926. Films include *The Two Orphans* (1911), *The Spoilers* (1914), *The Rosary* (1915), *The Cost of Hatred* (1917), *The Spanish Dancer* (1923), *Our Dancing Daughters* (1928), and *Rendezvous at Midnight* (1935; her last film).   **506. Lois Wilson** (1898–1988). One of the most charming of Paramount contract stars, but seldom given the roles that she deserved, Lois Wilson was at her best in *Miss Lulu Bett* (1921). In films from the mid-'teens through the late forties. Films include *What Every Woman Knows* (1921), *Manslaughter* (1922), *The Covered Wagon* (1923), *Monsieur Beaucaire* (1924), *The Vanishing American* (1925), *Irish Luck* (1925), and *The Great Gatsby* (1926). **507. Margery Wilson** (1896–1986). A D. W. Griffith discovery, who made her debut in *Intolerance* (1916). Marjorie Wilson was a multi-talented individual, equally at ease acting, directing, or writing. Films include *The Habit of Happiness* (1916), *The Primal Lure* (1916), *The Desert Man* (1917), *Wolf Lowry* (1917), *Venus in the East* (1919), and *That Something* (1921). Autobiography: *I Found My Way* (Philadelphia: Lippincott, 1956).

506

507

508

509

510

508. Claire Windsor (1898–1972). A discovery of director Lois Weber in whose films *To Please One Woman* (1920), *What's Worth While* (1921), *Too Wise Wives* (1921), *The Blot* (1921), and *What Do Men Want?* (1921) Claire Windsor was at her best, playing with quiet understatement. Films include *Little Church Around the Corner* (1923), *Rupert of Hentzau* (1923), *Dance Madness* (1926), *The Claw* (1927), and *Captain Lash* (1929).   **509. Jane Winton** (1905–1959). A patrician, English-looking actress of the late twenties, Jane Winton looked her best in costume pictures. Films include *Tomorrow's Love* (1925), *My Old Dutch* (1925), *Don Juan* (1926), *The Beloved Rogue* (1927), *Sunrise — A Song of Two Humans* (1927), and *The Patsy* (1928).   **510. Louis Wolheim** (1880–1931). Eugene O'Neill's *The Hairy Ape* (stage, 1922) was on screen from 1914 through 1931 and memorable as Katczinsky in *All Quiet on the Western Front* (1930). Films include *The Sunbeam* (1916), *The Avenging Trail* (1917), *Dr. Jekyll and Mr. Hyde* (1920), *Orphans of the Storm* (1921), *Sherlock Holmes* (1922), *America* (1924), *Two Arabian Knights* (1927), and *Tempest* (1928).

511

512

513

511. Anna May Wong (1905–1961). The only Chinese-American performer to enjoy a major career in silent Hollywood films (and in European productions), Anna May Wong was a Santa Monica, California, schoolgirl who came to prominence with an exquisitely sensitive and underplayed performance in the first two-color Technicolor feature: *The Toll of the Sea* (1922). Films include *Bits of Life* (1921), *Thundering Dawn* (1923), *Peter Pan* (1924), *Forty Winks* (1925), *A Trip to Chinatown* (1926), and *Mr. Wu* (1927).

512. Clara Kimball Young (1890–1960). An imposing actress, Clara Kimball Young seemed matronly even at the beginning of her career with Vitagraph in 1912. Films include *My Official Wife* (1914), *Trilby* (1915), *Camille* (1915), *The Foolish Virgin* (1916), *Cheating Cheaters* (1919), *Eyes of Youth* (1919), *The Worldly Madonna* (1922), and *Lying Wives* (1925). **513. Loretta Young** (1913–). A silent ingénue in starring roles from 1928, Loretta Young developed into a very good actress in the thirties, but later she began to take herself too seriously. Films include *The Whip Woman* (1928), *Laugh, Clown, Laugh* (1928), and *The Magnificent Flirt* (1928).

THE SILENT STAR:
A GENERAL
BIBLIOGRAPHY

"Actresses Must Be Young." *The Moving Picture World*, 27 December 1913, p. 1556.

Agnew, Francis. *Motion Picture Acting*. New York: Reliance Newspaper Syndicate, 1913.

Bartlett, Randolph. "The Star Idea versus the Star System." *Motion Picture Magazine*, August 1919, pp. 36-37, 107.

Carr, Harry C. "How Griffith Picks His Leading Women." *Photoplay*, December 1918, pp. 24-25.

Carroll, David. *The Matinee Idols*. New York: Arbor, 1972.

Coxhead, Elizabeth. "Film Actor." *Close Up*, March 1933, pp. 47-49.

Douglass, Charles A., Jr. *Motion Picture Stars*. Hollywood: The Stars' Co., 1928.

Fox, Charles Donald, *Famous Film Folk: A Gallery of Life Portraits and Biographies*. New York: George H. Doran Company, 1925.

————, and Milton L. Silver. *Who's Who on the Screen*. New York: Ross Publishing Company, 1920.

Graham, Charles. "Acting for the Films in 1912." *Sight and Sound*, Autumn 1935, pp. 118-119.

Griffith, David W. "What I Demand of Movie Stars." *Motion Picture Classic*, February 1917, pp. 40-41, 68.

Harrison, Louis Reeves. "The Player." *The Moving Picture World*, September 20, 1913, p. 1260.

Head, June. *Star Gazing*. London: Peter Davies, 1931.

Herman, Hal C., editor. *How I Broke into the Movies*. Hollywood: The Author, 1928.

Jones, Henry Arthur. "Heroines of the Film." *Living Age*, 15 October 1921, pp. 176-179.

Justice, Fred C., and Tom R. Smith, editors and compilers. *Who's Who in the Film World*. Los Angeles: Film World Publishing Company, 1914.

Kerr, Walter. *The Silent Clowns*. New York: Alfred A. Knopf, 1975.

Kitchell, William H. "The Artists of the Screen." *The Moving Picture World*, 30 September 1911, p. 949.

Klumph, Inez and Helen. *Screen Acting: Its Requirements and Rewards*. New York: Falk Publishing Company, 1922.

Lahue, Kalton C., and Samuel Gill. *Clown Princes and Court Jesters: Some Great Comics of the Silent Screen*. South Brunswick, NJ: A. S. Barnes, 1970.

Lowrey, Carolyn. *The First One Hundred Noted Men and Women of the Screen*. New York: Moffat, Yard, 1920.

Macgowan, Kenneth. "Stage Stars Who Made Good on Screen." *Dramatic Mirror*, 15 February 1919, p. 229.

Marple, Albert. "The Character Man of the Movies." *Motion Picture Classic*, February 1916, pp. 33-35.

Marsh, Mae. *Screen Acting*. Los Angeles: Photo-Star Publishing Company, 1921.

McDonald, Gerald D. "Origin of the Star System." *Films in Review*, vol. IV, no. 9, November 1953, pp. 449-458.

———. "From Stage to Screen." *Films in Review*, vol. VI, no. 1, January 1955, pp. 13-18.

Meridan, Oscar. "Confessions of a Star." *Photoplay*, September 1915, pp. 139-143.

Motion Picture Studio Directory. New York: Motion Picture News, 1916-1924.

Parker, David L. "Famous Players in Peril: When the Stage Stars of the Mid 'Teens Made Movies." *Views and Reviews*, vol. IV, no. 2, Winter 1972, pp. 97-100.

Potamkin, Harry Alan. "The Personality of the Player: A Phase of Unity." *Close Up*, April 1930, pp. 290-297.

Quirk, James R. "Star Dust." *Photoplay*, June 1918, pp. 18-20.

Sherwood, Robert E. "The Perils of Monotony." *Photoplay*, November 1925, pp. 70, 123.

Slide, Anthony. *The Griffith Actresses*. New York: A. S. Barnes, 1975.

———. "The Evolution of the Film Star." *Aspects of American Film History Prior to 1920*. Metuchen, NJ: Scarecrow Press, 1978, pp. 1-6.

Spears, Jack. *Hollywood: The Golden Era*. South Brunswick, NJ: A. S. Barnes, 1971.

Stewart, William T., Arthur F. McClure, and Ken D. Jones. *International Film Necrology*. New York: Garland, 1981.

Talmey, Allen. *Doug and Mary and Others*. New York: Macy-Masisu, 1927.

Tinee, Mae. *Life Stories of the Movies' Stars*. Hamilton OH: The Presto Publishing Company, 1916.

Wagenknecht, Edward. *The Movies in the Age of Innocence*. Norman OK: University of Oklahoma Press, 1962.

———. *Stars of the Silents*. Metuchen NJ: Scarecrow Press, 1987.

Walker, Alexander. *Stardom: The Hollywood Phenomenon*. New York: Stein and Day, 1970.

Weitzel, Edward. *Intimate Talks with Movie Stars*. New York: Dale Publishing Company, 1921.

Williamson, Mrs. Alice Muriel. *Alice in Movieland*. New York: Appleton, 1928.

Wright, Willard Huntington. "Peacocks of the Movies." *Photoplay*, December 1919, pp. 44-46. (Author better known under pseudonym of S. S. Van Dine)

Zierold, Norman. *Sex Goddesses of the Silent Screen*. Chicago: Regnery, 1973.

SILENT PORTRAITS
Stars of the Silent Screen in
Historic Photographs

Composed by Eastern Graphics, Binghamton,
New York. Text typeset in 10-point Cochin
with display lines in Benguiat Gothic.
Cover design by Katha Fauty.
Printed by Johnson City Publishing,
Binghamton, New York.